SENSORDEVICES 2022

The Thirteenth International Conference on Sensor Device Technologies and Applications

October 16 - 20, 2022

Lisbon, Portugal

SENSORDEVICES 2022 Editors

Manuela Vieira, Instituto Superior de Engenharia de Lisboa (ISEL) and CTS-UNINOVA, Portugal

Printed from e-media with permission by:

Curran Associates, Inc.
57 Morehouse Lane
Red Hook, NY 12571

Some format issues inherent in the e-media version may also appear in this print version.

Printed with permission by Curran Associates, Inc. (2023)

International Academy, Research, and Industry Association (IARIA)
412 Derby Way
Wilmington, DE 19810

Phone: (408) 893-6407
Fax: (408) 527-6351

petre@iaria.org

Additional copies of this publication are available from:

Curran Associates, Inc.
57 Morehouse Lane
Red Hook, NY 12571 USA
Phone: 845-758-0400
Fax: 845-758-2633
Email: curran@proceedings.com
Web: www.proceedings.com

Table of Contents

Ultra-Thin Platinum Hydrogen Sensors with a Twin-T Filter Circuit for Electrical Control of Sensitivity 1
Shoki Wakabayashi, Takahiro Mori, Jin Wang, Kenji Sakai, and Toshihiko Kiwa

Adaptive Traffic Control Through Visible Light Communication 3
Manuel Vieira, Manuela Vieira, Paula Louro, and Pedro Vieira

VLC Based Guidance System to Be Used by Mobile Users Inside Large Buildings 9
Manuela Vieira, Manuel Vieira, Paula Louro, Alessandro Fantoni, and Pedro Vieira

Impact of Packaging on the Static Behavior of Piezoresitive Pressure Sensor Dedicated to Blast Wave Monitoring 15
Bilel Achour, Lilian Marty, Kevin Sanchez, Samuel Charlot, Xavier Dollat, Benjamin Reig, Laurent Bouscayrol, Aurelie Lecestre, Anthony Coustou, Andre Ferrand, Herve Aubert, and Patrick Pons

Positioning Using Visible Light Communication Footprints 21
Paula Louro, Manuela Vieira, Manuel Augusto Vieira, and Pedro Vieira

Simultaneous Localization, Mapping and Moving-Object Tracking Using Helmet-Mounted LiDAR for Micro-Mobility 25
Ibuki Yoshida, Akihiko Yoshida, Masafumi Hashimoto, and Kazuhiko Takahashi

Acoustic Emission Sensing of Materials and Structures 32
Irinela Chilibon

Experimental Comparison of Vital Sign Extraction Using Off-The-Shelf MIMO FMCW Radar at Different Angles 38
Shahzad Ahmed, Junbyung Park, Chanwoo Choi, and Sung Ho Cho

Fluorescence Assay for Spore Germination Detection 41
Andreas Tortschanoff, Sabine Lengger, Gerald Aubock, and Cristina Consani

Towards Safety Methods for Unmanned Aerial Systems to achieve Fail-Safe or Fail-Operational Behaviour 43
Philipp Stelzer, Raphael Schermann, Felix Warmer, Hannes Winkler, Georg Macher, and Christian Steger

A High Purity Fused Silica (HPFS) Glass Substrate based 77 GHz 4 × 4 Butler Matrix for Automotive Radars 51
Ronak Sakhiya and Sazzadur Chowdhury

Development of Sensor Devices for Structural Health Monitoring of Buildings and Civil Infrastructures 57
Narito Kurata

SENSORDEVICES 2022

Forward

The Thirteenth International Conference on Sensor Device Technologies and Applications (SENSORDEVICES 2022), held on October 16-20, 2022, continued a series of events focusing on sensor devices themselves, the technology-capturing style of sensors, special technologies, signal control and interfaces, and particularly sensors-oriented applications. The evolution of the nano-and microtechnologies, nanomaterials, and the new business services make the sensor device industry and research on sensor-themselves very challenging.

Most of the sensor-oriented research and industry initiatives are focusing on sensor networks, data security, exchange protocols, energy optimization, and features related to intermittent connections. Recently, the concept of Internet-of-things gathers attention, especially when integrating IPv4 and IIPv6 networks. We welcomed technical papers presenting research and practical results, position papers addressing the pros and cons of specific proposals, such as those being discussed in the standard fora or in industry consortia, survey papers addressing the key problems and solutions on any of the above topics short papers on work in progress, and panel proposals.

We take here the opportunity to warmly thank all the members of the SENSORDEVICES 2022 technical program committee, as well as all the reviewers. The creation of such a high quality conference program would not have been possible without their involvement. We also kindly thank all the authors who dedicated much of their time and effort to contribute to SENSORDEVICES 2022. We truly believe that, thanks to all these efforts, the final conference program consisted of top quality contributions.

We also thank the members of the SENSORDEVICES 2022 organizing committee for their help in handling the logistics and for their work that made this professional meeting a success.

We hope that SENSORDEVICES 2022 was a successful international forum for the exchange of ideas and results between academia and industry and to promote further progress in the area of sensor devices technologies and applications. We also hope that Lisbon provided a pleasant environment during the conference and everyone saved some time to enjoy the historic charm of the city.

SENSORDEVICES 2022 Chairs

SENSORDEVICES 2022 Steering Committee

Arcady Zhukov, University of Basque Country (UPV/EHU), San Sebastian / Ikerbasque, Basque Foundation for Science, Bilbao, Spain
Narito Kurata, Tsukuba University of Technology, Japan
Sazzadur Chowdhury. University of Windsor, Canada
Manuela Vieira, CTS/ISEL/IPL, Portugal

SENSORDEVICES 2022 Publicity Chair

Sandra Viciano Tudela, Universitat Politecnica de Valencia, Spain
Jose Luis García, Universitat Politecnica de Valencia, Spain

SENSORDEVICES 2022

Committee

SENSORDEVICES 2022 Steering Committee

SENSORDEVICES 2022 Publicity Chair

SENSORDEVICES 2022 Technical Program Committee

Copyright Information

Ultra-Thin Platinum Hydrogen Sensors with a Twin-T Filter Circuit for Electrical Control of Sensitivity

Shoki Wakabayashi, Takahiro Mori, Jin Wang, Kenji Sakai, Toshihiko Kiwa
Graduate School Interdisciplinary Science and Engineering in Health Systems
Okayama University
3-1-1 Tsushima-naka, Kita-ku, Okayama 700-8530, Japan
E-mail: pgju8212@s.okayama-u.ac.jp, p7lz3cav@s.okayama-u.ac.jp, wangjin@okayama-u.ac.jp, sakai-k@okayama-u.ac.jp, kiwa@okayama-u.ac.jp

Abstract— **A twin-T type notch filter ultra-thin hydrogen sensor has been developed to improve and control the sensitivity of the sensors. The ultra-thin platinum films were used as resistors of a twin-T notch filter, so the frequency properties of the filter change when the resistivity of the films changes by hydrogen gas exposer. Therefore, the amplitude of output signals depends on the operation frequency of the sensor. The change in the output signal of the fabricated sensor for 1%-hydrogen gas exposure was 2.9% at 1.19 kHz and 4.3% at 0.99 kHz. This result indicates that the sensitivity of the sensor could be electrically controlled by changing the operating frequency of the sensor.**

Keywords-hydrogen; sensor; ultra-thin film; twin-T; notch filter; platinum.

I. INTRODUCTION

A large amount of greenhouse gas emission from using fossil fuels cause global warming. Progressing global warming is the serious problem because that leads to environmental destruction and abnormal weather. Therefore, renewable energy is attracting attention as a new energy souse to reduce the amount of greenhouse gas. Especially, hydrogen energy is expected because the energy has the high efficiency, and the supply of the energy is stable. However, hydrogen gas (H_2) easily leaks and explodes, so the early detection of H_2 with hydrogen sensors is required for using hydrogen energy safely. Up to now, various types of hydrogen sensors, including a Catalytic-Combustion (CC) type, a Field-Effect Transistor (FET) type, and a Resistance Change (RC) type have been developed. A CC type sensor measures change in the temperature of a catalytic metal film, e.g., platinum (Pt) and palladium (Pd) by exposure to H_2. Detection with a CC type sensor is less affected by ambient conditions such as temperature and humidity. However, a CC type sensor generally operates at high temperature comparing to the other types of sensors [1-2]. So, a CC type sensor requires higher energy consumption for warming the sensor by a heater. On the other hand, a FET type sensor can operate at lower temperature. This type of sensor does not require the warming by heater, so this type of sensor can operate with lower energy consumption. A FET type sensor measures change in the work function of the catalytic metal film fabricated on the gate electrode of FET. The FET type sensor has relatively high sensitivity. However, a FET type sensor requires complicated fabrication process in a clean room [3]. The RC type sensor consists of Pd thin films on a substrate, so the fabrication process is simpler than a FET type sensor. The volume of Pd increases by absorption of H_2 into the Pd, and the resistance of the Pd changes. Thus, this type of sensor measures change in the resistance of Pd. However, the volume of Pd films change by absorption and dissociation of H_2, so Pd films irreversibly degrade [4].

In our group, a Pt ultra-thin film hydrogen sensor has been proposed and developed [5-7]. Pt film does not absorb H_2, so this type of sensor is more durable against H_2. H_2 is dissociated on the surface of Pt films, and electrons are injected into the films. Thus, the resistance of Pt films decreases while the resistivity of Pd films increases. The selectivity of similar sensor was measured at room temperature and reported elsewhere. This sensor could detect H_2 with a concentration of above 0.1 % [8].

II. METHODOLOGY

Figure 1 shows (a) the structure of the hydrogen sensor and (b) the equivalent circuit of twin-T. The Pt ultra-thin film hydrogen sensor had three layers of silicon, titanium nitride (TiN), and Pt. TiN and Pt were formed on a silicon substrate by the sputtering method. The thickness of TiN was 20 nm and that of Pt was 10 nm.

In this study, the Pt ultra-thin films hydrogen sensors were integral ted into a twin-T type notch filter circuits as resistors. A twin-T circuit has the feature that the output signals reduce at a specific frequency (notch frequency). The notch frequency (f_n) can be given by

$$f_n = \frac{1}{2\pi CR}, \tag{1}$$

where, C is capacity, and R is resistance. Like the ultra-thin films hydrogen sensors mentioned above, the resistance decreases with increasing the concentration of H_2. Since the Pt films consists of resistive part of the circuit R, the notch frequency shifts by exposure to H_2. Figure 2 shows the schematic illustration of the frequency dependence of the amplitude and phases before and after hydrogen exposure. The notch frequency slightly increases with the exposure. Thus, concentration of H_2 could be measured by measuring the amplitude and/or phase of the output signals (V_{out}) operating at the frequency ($f_o \approx f_n$). The sensitivity (S) can be given by

$$S = \left.\frac{dV_{out}}{df}\right|_{f=f_n} \tag{2}$$

Because the sensitivity depends on the differential of the properties along with the frequency, the sensitivity of this type of sensor could be electrically controlled by changing the operation frequency.

III. EXPRIMENTS AND RESULTS

Figure 3 shows the change in the amplitude and phase of the output signals as time at 1.19 kHz which was the notch frequency of the circuit without hydrogen exposure. The sensor was exposed to gas balanced by 20%-oxygen and 80%-nitrogen gas (Air) for 5 min and 1%-hydrogen gas of whose pressure balanced by 20%-oxygen and 80%-nitrogen gas to be 1 atm for 5 min. The change in amplitude and phase were 2.8 % and 4.8 deg.

Figure 4 shows the change in the amplitude and phase of the output signals as a function of the operating frequency of the circuit when the sensor was exposed to 1%-hydrogen gas. The change rates depend on the operation frequencies and maximize at the frequency of 0.99 kHz and 1.19 kHz for the amplitude and the phase, respectively. The corresponding changing rates were 4.3% and 2.9%. This result clearly indicates that the sensitivity of the sensor could be electrically controlled by changing the operating frequency.

IV. CONCLUSION

In our group, the ultra-thin Pt hydrogen sensor was developed using the twin-T circuit. The sensor could be electrically controlled by changing the operating frequency. The variation of sensor properties by the fabrication process can be reduced, therefore, a series of sensors with a uniform sensitivity can be realized.

REFERENCES

[1] V.R. Katti, A.K. Dehnath, S.C. Gadkari, S.K. Gupta, and V.C. Sahni," Passivated thick film catalytic type H2 sensor operating at low temperature," Sens. Actuators B, 84, pp. 219-225, 2002.

[2] M.G. Jones and T.G. Nevell," The detection of hydrogen using catalytic flammable gas sensors," Sens. Actuators, 16, pp. 215-224, 1989.

[3] H.Fukuda and Y.Tada, "Response to Hydrogen in Field-effect Transistor Sensor with Platinum Nanoparticles," Muroran Institute of Technology Academic Resources Archive, 69, pp 77-83, 2020.

[4] B.D.Adams and A.Chen, "The role of palladium in a hydrogen economy," Materials Today, Volume 14, Issue 6, pp. 282-289, 2011.

[5] K.Tsukada, S.Takeichi, K.Sakai, and T. Kiwa, "Ultrathin-film hydrogen gas sensor with nanostructurally modified surface," Japanese Journal of Applied Physics, .Volume 53, pp. 076701 1-4, 2014

[6] K. Tsukada, H. Inoue, F. Katayama, K. Sakai, and T. Kiwa, "Changes in Work Function and Electrical Resistance of Pt Thin Films in the Presence of Hydrogen Gas," Jpn. J. Appl. Phys., Volume 51, pp. 015701 1-4, 2012.

[7] K.Tsukada, et al. "A study of fast response characteristics for hydrogen sensing with platinum FET sensor," Sensors and Actuators B: Chemical, Volume 114, Issue 1, pp.158-163, 2006.

[8] T.Mori, et al. "Study on the Performance of Sensitive Part of Bridge Type Ultra-thin Film Hydrogen Sensor," presented at The Twelfth International Conference On Sensor Device Technologies And Applications, SENSORDEVICE 2021 Nov 14-18, 2021

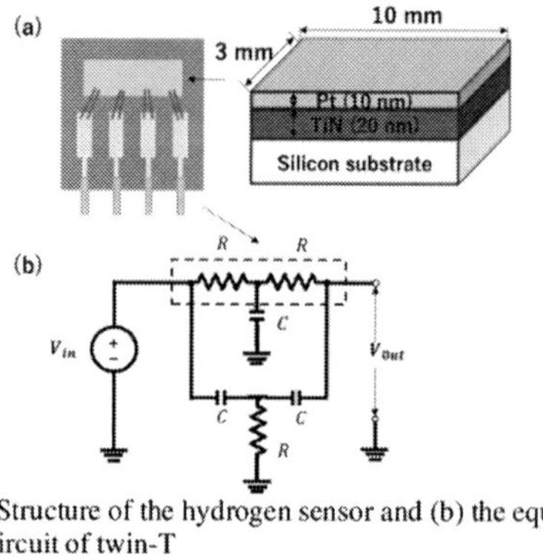

Figure 1. (a) Structure of the hydrogen sensor and (b) the equivalent circuit of twin-T

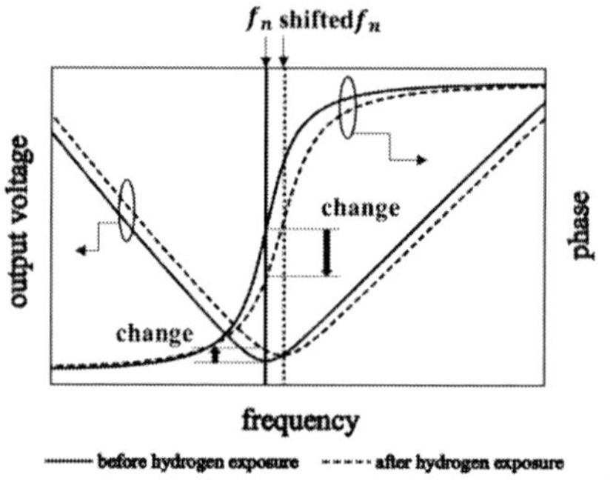

Figure 2. The schematic illustration of the frequency dependence of the amplitude and phase before and after hydrogen exposure

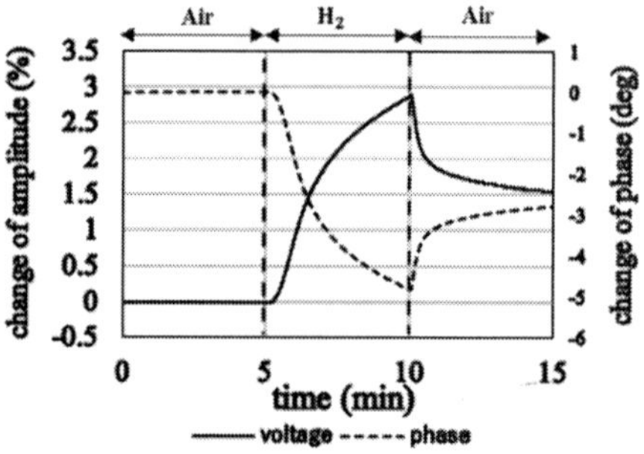

Figure 3. The change in the amplitude and phase of the output signals as time at 1.19 kHz which was the notch frequency of the circuit without hydrogen exposure.

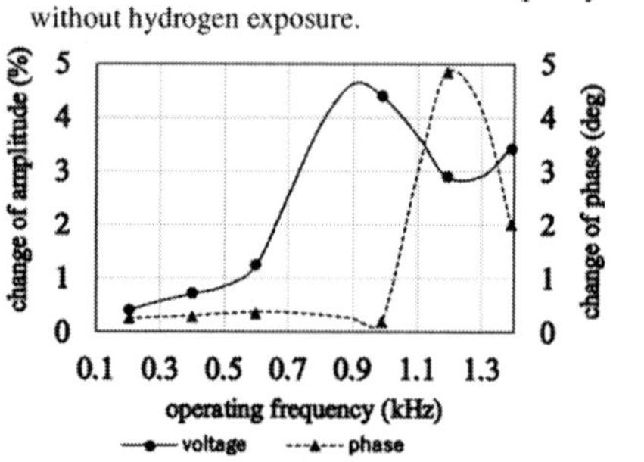

Figure 4. The change in the amplitude and phase of the output signals as a function of the operating frequency of the circuit

Adaptive Traffic Control Through Visible Light Communication

Manuel Augusto Vieira, Manuela Vieira, Paula Louro,
ADETC/ISEL/IPL,
R. Conselheiro Emídio Navarro, 1959-007
Lisboa, Portugal
CTS-UNINOVA
Quinta da Torre, Monte da Caparica, 2829-516,
Caparica, Portugal

e-mail: mv@isel.pt, mv@isel- ipl.pt, plouro@deetc.isel.pt,

Pedro Vieira
ADETC/ISEL/IPL,
R. Conselheiro Emídio Navarro, 1959-007
Lisboa, Portugal
Instituto das Telecomunicações
Instituto Superior Técnico, 1049-001,
Lisboa, Portugal
e-mail: pvieira@isel.pt

Abstract— **Monitoring the network traffic status of urban roads in real-time can provide rich and high-quality basic data and allow the assessment of traffic control effects. Our work focuses on the use of Visible Light Communication (VLC) as a support for transmission of information providing guidance to drivers, as well as specific information to them. Connected vehicles communicate with one another and with the infrastructure using street lights, street lamps, and traffic signals. As a result of joint transmission, optical mobile receivers collect data, calculate their location for positioning, and, correspondingly, read transmitted data from each transmitter. As receivers and decoders, optical sensors with light filtering properties, are used. To command the passage of vehicles safely queue/request/response mechanisms and temporal/space relative pose concepts are used. The results indicate that the V-VLC system increases safety by directly monitoring critical points such as queue formation and dissipation, relative speed thresholds, as well as inter-vehicle spacing.**
.

Keywords- Adaptative Traffic control; Queue distance; Vehicle Pose Connectivity; Vehicular-Visible Light Communication (V-VLC); White LEDs, SiC photodetectors.

I. INTRODUCTION

The main objective of the Intelligent Transport System (ITS) technology is to optimize traffic safety and efficiency on public roads by increasing situation awareness and mitigating traffic accidents through vehicle-to-vehicle (V2V) and vehicle-to-infrastructure (V2I) communications [1] [2] [3]. By knowing, in real time, the location, speed and direction of nearby vehicles, a considerable improvement in traffic management is expected. The goal is to increase the safety and throughput of traffic intersections using cooperative driving [4].

The traffic data collected by the current traffic control system using induction loop detector and other existing sensors is limited. With the advancement of the wireless communication technologies and the development of the V2V and V2I systems, called Connected Vehicle, there is an opportunity to optimize the operation of urban traffic network by cooperation between traffic signal control and driving behaviors. In this area, Visible Light Communication (VLC) has a great potential for applications due to their relatively simple design for basic functioning, efficiency, and large geographical distribution. VLC is an emerging technology [5] that enables data communication by modulating information on the intensity of the light emitted by LEDs. In the case of vehicular communications, the use of VLC is made easier because all vehicles, street lights, and traffic lights are equipped with LEDs, using them for illumination, enabling the dual use of exterior automotive and infrastructure lighting for both illumination and communication purposes [6].

The adaptive traffic control strategy aims to respond to real-time traffic demand through current and predicted traffic flow data modeling. The adaptive traffic control system in a vehicle-to-everything (V2X) environment can collect more detailed information than the fixed coil detector, such as vehicle position, speed, queue length, and stopping time. While V2V links are particularly important for safety functionalities, such as pre-crash sensing and forward collision warning, I2V links provide the connected vehicles with a variety of useful information [7] [8].

Monitoring the network traffic status of urban roads in real-time can provide rich and high-quality basic data and allow the assessment of traffic control effects.

Our work focuses directly on the use of VLC as a support for the transmission of information providing guidance services and specific information to drivers. This paper is organized as follows. After the introduction, in Section 2, the V-VLC communication link is described and the scenario, architecture, communication protocol, coding/decoding techniques analyzed. In Section 3, the experimental results are reported and the system evaluation performed. A phasing traffic flow diagram based on V-VLC is developed, as a Proof of Concept (PoC). Finally, in Section 4, the main conclusions are presented.

II. V-VLC COMMUNICATION LINK

In this section, the transmitter and receiver of the proposed adaptive traffic control system are investigated concretely. The adaptive model is introduced specifically.

A. *System Design*

A V-VLC system consists of a transmitter to generate modulated light and a receiver to detect the received light variation located at the infrastructures and at the driving cars. Both the transmitter and the receiver are connected through the wireless channel.

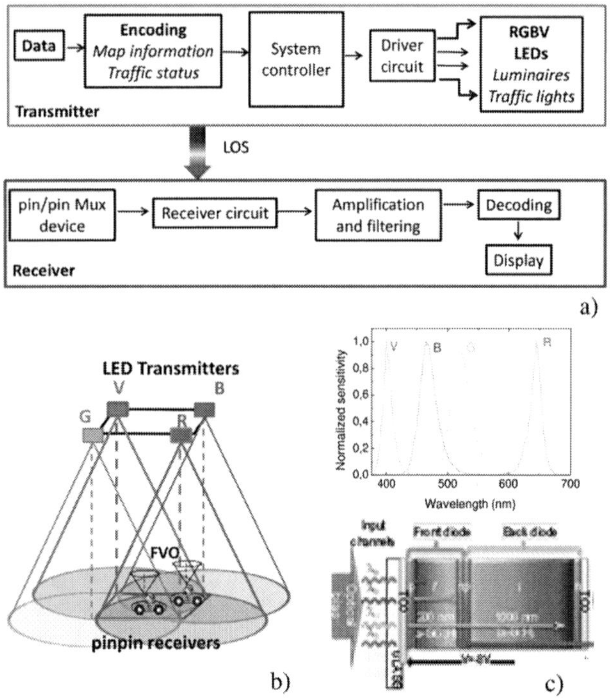

Figure 1. a) Block diagram of a VLC Communication link. b) Transmitters and receivers 3D relative positions. c) Spectra of the input channels and configuration and operation of the pin/pin Mux device

Figure 1 illustrates the basic architecture of a VLC system. Both communication modules are software defined, where modulation/ demodulation can be programed.The VLC emitter has a dual purpose, emits light, and transmits data instantaneously by using the same optical power without any noticeable flickering. The digital VLC emitter module converts the binary data to intensity modulated light waves for transmission. A driving circuit controls the switching of the LED according to the incoming binary data at the given data rate, generating an amplitude modulated light beam. Here, the light produced by the LED is modulated with ON–OFF-keying (OOK) amplitude modulation [9].

White light tetra-chromatic sources are used providing a different data channel for each chip. Each luminaire is composed of four white WLEDs framed at the corners of a square (see Figure 1b). They consist of red, green, blue and violet chips and combine the lights in correct proportion to generate white light. At each node, only one chip of the LED is modulated for data transmission, the Red (R: 626 nm), the Green (G: 530 nm), the Blue (B: 470 nm) or the Violet (V). Modulation and digital-to-analog conversion of the information bits is done using signal processing techniques. Parasitic capacitance (traces and support circuitry) plays an important role in increasing the RC time constant and thus slowing transitions. However, the typical bit rates that can be supported by fast moving vehicles is usually limited by channel conditions, not by the switching speed of the LED.

The visible light emitted by the LEDs passes through the transmission medium and is received by the *MUX* photodetector that acts as an active filter for the visible region of the light spectrum [10]. The device operation is displayed in Figure 1c. Independent tuning of each channel is performed by steady state violet optical bias superimposed from the front side of the device. The generated photocurrent is measured at -8V. The MUX photodetector multiplexes the different optical channels, perform different filtering processes (amplification, switching, and wavelength conversion) and decode the encoded signals, recovering the transmitted information.

The LEDs are modeled as Lambertian sources where the luminance is distributed uniformly in all directions, whereas the luminous intensity is different in all directions [11]. The coverage map for a square unit cell is displayed in Figure 2. All the values were converted to decibel (dB).The nine possible overlaps (#1-#9), defined as fingerprint regions, as well as the possible receiver orientations (steering angles; δ) are also pointed out for the unit square cell.

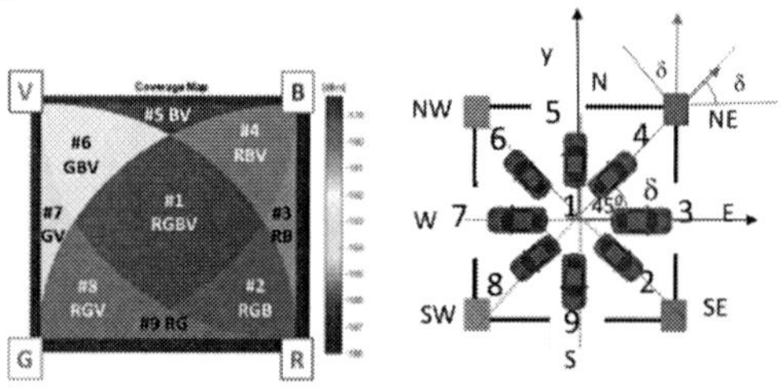

Figure 2. Illustration of the coverage map in the unit cell: footprint regions (#1-#9) and steering angle codes (2-9).

The received channel can be expresssed as $y=\mu hx+n$ where y represents the received signal, x the transmitted signal, μ is the photoelectric conversion factor which can be normalized as $\mu = 1$, h is the channel gain and n is the additive white Gaussian noise of which the mean is 0. The responsivity of the receiver depends on its physical structure and on the effective area collection. After receiving the signal, it is in turn filtered, amplified, and converted back to digital format for demodulation. The received signal power includes both the energy transmitted from the transmitter and from ambient light. The device receives multiple signals, finds the centroid of the received coordinates, and stores it as the reference point position. Nine reference points, for each unit cell, are identified giving a fine-grained resolution in the localization of the mobile device across each cell (see Figure 2). The input of the guidance system is the coded signal sent by the transmitters to an identify vehicle (I2V), and includes its position in the network $P(x_i, y_j)$, inside the unit cell (#1-#9) and the steering angle, δ (2-9) that guides the driver orientation across his path.

B. Scenario and Architecture

The typical single intersection (four-legged intersection) is attached to sixteen roads, eight incoming from and eight outgoing to North, West, South, and East neighbor crossroads' roads. The simulated scenario is a traffic light controlled intersection as displayed in Figure 3.

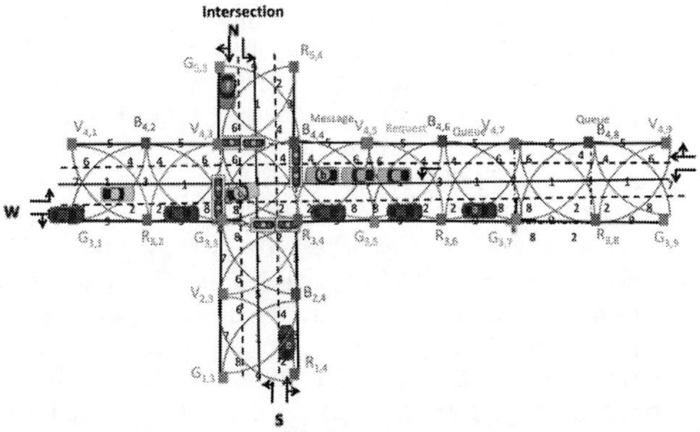

Figure 3. Simulated scenario. V2X optical infrastructure and generated joint footprints in a split crossroad (LED array=RGBV color spots).

Four traffic flows were considered. One is coming from West (W) with seven vehicles approaching the crossroad: five a_i Vehicles with straight movement and three c_i Vehicles with left turn only. In the second flow, three b_i Vehicles from East (E) approach the intersection with left turn only. In the third flow, *e* Vehicle, oncoming from South (S), has right-turn approach. Finally, in the fourth flow, *f* Vehicle coming from North, goes straight. Road request and response segments, offer a binary (turn left / straight or turn right) choice.

An orthogonal topology based on clusters of square unit cells was considered. The grid size was chosen in order to avoid an overlap in the receiver from the data in adjacent grid points. Each transmitter, $X_{i,j}$, carries its own color, X, (RGBV) as well as its horizontal and vertical ID position in the surrounding network (i,j). In the PoC, was assumed that the crossroad is located in the intersections of line 4 with column 3. The emitters (street lamps) are located at the nodes along the roadside. Thus, each LED sends a I2V message that includes the synchronism, its physical ID and the traffic information. When a probe vehicle enters the streetlight´s capture range, the receiver replies to the light signal, and assigns a unique ID and the traffic message.

Figure 4, presents a draft of a mesh cellular hybrid structure that can be used to create a gateway-free system.

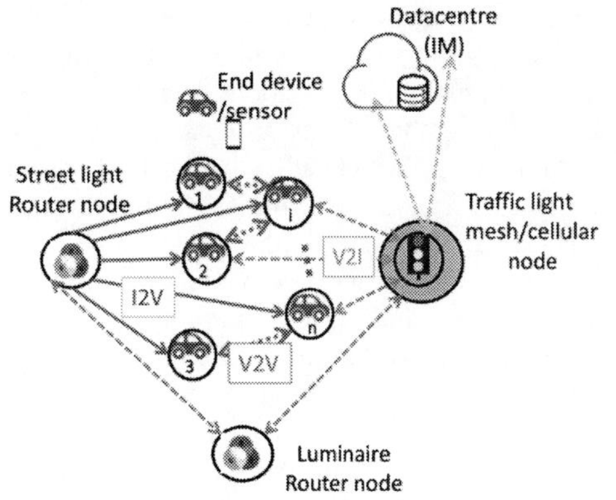

Figure 4. Mesh and cellular hybrid architecture.

The street lights are equipped with one of two types of nodes: A "mesh" controller that connects with other nodes in its vicinity. These controllers can forward messages to the vehicles (I2V) in the mesh, acting like routers nodes in the network. The other one is the "mesh/cellular" hybrid controller that is also equipped with a modem provides IP base connectivity to the Intersection Manager (IM) services. These nodes act as border-router and can be used for edge computing [12]. This architecture enables edge computing and device-to-cloud communication (I2IM), and enable peer-to-peer communication (I2I), to exchange information. It performs much of the processing on embedded computing platforms, directly interfacing to sensors and controllers. It supports geo-distribution, local decision making, and real-time load-balancing.

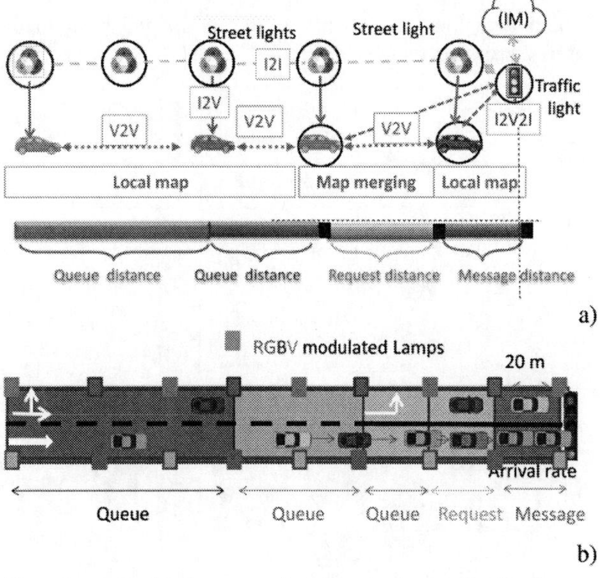

Figure 5. a) Graphical representation of the simultaneous localization as a function of node density, mobility and transmission range. b) Design of the state representation in the west arm of the intersection, with cells length.

As exemplified in Figure 5, the vehicle movement along the road can be thought as a queue, where the vehicles arrive at a lane, wait if the lane is congested and then move once the congestion reduces. For the intersection manager crossing coordination, the vehicle and the IM exchange information through two types of messages, "request" (V2I) and "response" (I2V). Inside the request distance, an approach "request" is sent, using as emitter the headlights. The "request" contains all the information that is necessary for a vehicle's space-time reservation for its intersection crossing (speeds, and flow directions). IM uses this information to convert it in a sequence of timed rectangular spaces that each assigned vehicle needs to occupy the intersection. The objective is to let the IM knows the position of vehicles inside the environment at each step t

A highly congested traffic scenario will be strongly connected. In order to determine the delay, the number of vehicles queuing in each cell at the beginning and end of the green time is determined by V2V2I observation, as illustrated in Figure 5a. An IM acknowledge is sent, "response" from the traffic signal over the facing receiver to the in car application of the head vehicle. Once the response is received (message distance in Figure 5, the vehicle is required to follow the provided occupancy trajectories (footprint regions, see Figure 2). If a request has any potential risk of collision with all other vehicles that have already been approved to cross the intersection, the control manager only sends back to the vehicle (V2I) the "response" after the risk of conflict is exceeded.

C. *Color Phasing diagram*

A color phasing diagram for a four-legged intersection is shown in Figure 6. We have assumed four "color poses" linked with the radial range of the modulated light in the RGBV crossroad nodes [13].

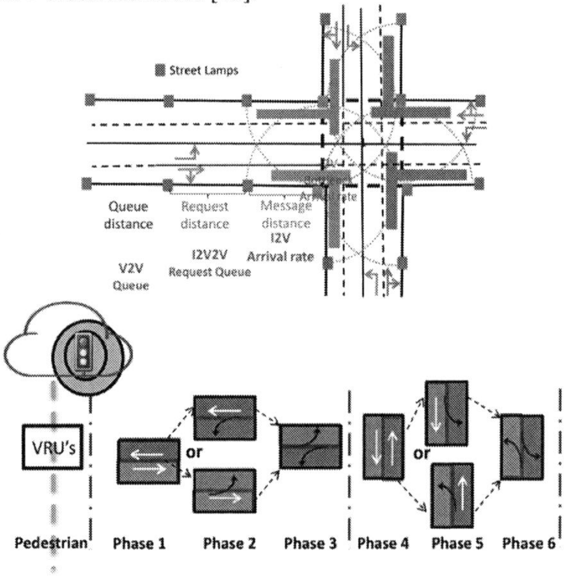

Figure 6. Phasing diagram in a four-legged intersection.

The West straight, South left turn and West right turn maneuvers correspond to the" Green poses". "Red poses" are related to South straight, East left turn, and South right turn maneuvers. "Blue poses" are related to East straight, North left turn, and East right turn maneuvers, and "violet poses" are related to North straight, West left turn, and North right turn maneuvers.

D. *Multi-Vehicle Cooperative Localization*

There are critical points where traffic conditions change: the point at which a vehicle begins to decelerate when the traffic light turns red (message distance), the point at which it stops and joins the queue (queue distance), the point at which it starts to accelerate when the traffic light turns green (request distance) or the points at which the coming vehicle is slowed by the leaving vehicle. With V2I2V communication, the travel time that influences traffic channelization in different routes can be calculated and real-time data about speed, spacing, queues, and saturation can be collected across the queue, request and message distances. In Figure 7, the movement of the cars in successive moments is depicted with their colored poses (colored arrows) and $q_{i,j}$ spatial relative poses (dot line).

We denote $q(t)$, $q(t')$, $q(t'')$, $q(t''')$ as the vehicle pose estimation at the time t, t', t'', t''' (request, response, enter and exit times), respectively. All the requests contain vehicle positions and approach speeds. If followers exist the request message from its leader includes the position and speed previously received by V2V. This information alerts the controller to a later request message (V2I), confirmed by the follow vehicle. In the PoC we have assumed that $t_{a1}<t_{b1}<t_{a2}<t_{b2}<t_{a3}<t_{c1}<t_{b3}<t_e<t_{a4}<t_{c2}<t_{a5}<t_f$.

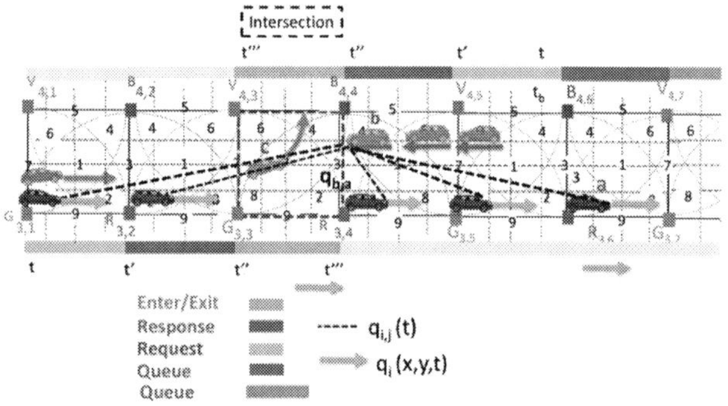

Figure 7 Movement of the cars, in the successive moments, with their colorful poses (color arrows) and $q_{i,j}$ spatial relative poses (dot lines).

The vehicle speed can be calculated by measuring the actual travelled distance overtime, using the ID´s transmitters tracking. The receivers compute the geographical position in the successive instants (path) and infer the vehicle's speed. When two vehicles are in neighborhood and in different lanes, the geometric relationship between them ($q_{i,j}$) can be inferred fusing their self-localizations via a chain of geometric relationships among the vehicles poses and the local maps. For a vehicle with several neighboring vehicles, the mesh node uses the indirect V2V relative pose estimations method taking advantage of the data of each neighboring vehicle [13].

III. EXPERIMENTAL EVALUATION

A. *Communication Protocol and Coding/Decoding Techniques*

To code the information, an On-Off keying (OOK) modulation scheme was used and it was considered a synchronous transmission based on a 64- bits data frame. The frame is divided into four, if the transmitter is a streetlamp or headlamp, or five blocks, if the transmitter is the traffic light. The first block is the synchronization block [10101], the last is the payload data (traffic message) and a stop bit ends the frame. The second block, the ID block gives the location (*x, y* coordinates) of the emitters inside the array ($X_{i,j}$). Cell's IDs are encoded using a 4 bits binary representation for the decimal number. The δ block (steering angle (δ)) completes the pose in a frame time $q(x,y,\ \delta,\ t)$. Eight steering angles along the cardinal points and coded with the same number of the footprints in the unit cell (Figure 2) are possible from a start point to the next goal. If the message is diffused by the IM transmitter, a pattern [0000] follows this identification, if it is a request (R) a pattern [00] is used. The traffic message completes the frame.

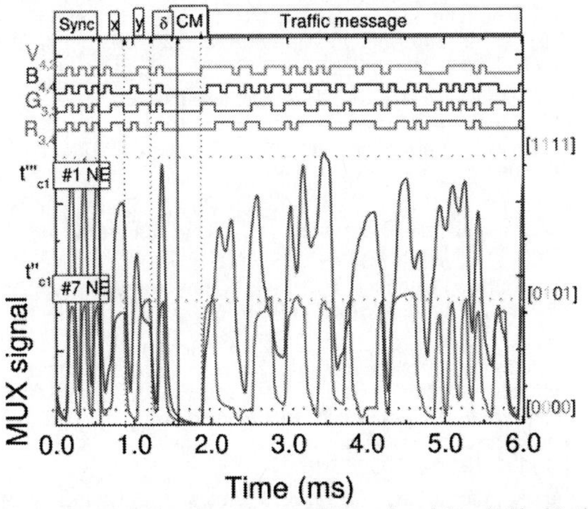

Figure 8 MUX signal responses and the assigned decoded inside the intersection; messages acquired by vehicle c_1, poses #7NE, #1NE. On the top the transmitted channels packets [R, G, B, V] are decoded.

Because the VLC has four independent emitters, the optical signal generated in the receiver can have one, two, three, or even four optical excitations, resulting in 2^4 different optical combinations and 16 different photocurrent levels at the photodetector. As an example, in Figure 8, two response MUX signals received by vehicle c_1 are displayed. This vehicle, driving on the left lane, receives order to enter the intersection in # 7, turning left (NE) and keeps moving in this direction across position #1 toward the North exit (Phase2, violet pose). In the right side, the received channels are identified by its 4-digit binary codes and associated positions in the unit cell. On the top the transmitted channels packets [R, G, B, V] are decoded.

B. *Adaptive Traffic Control*

In Figure 9, the normalized MUX signals and the decoded messages assigned to IM received by Vehicle a_1, b_1 at different response times are shown. On the top the transmitted channels [R, G, B, V] are decoded.

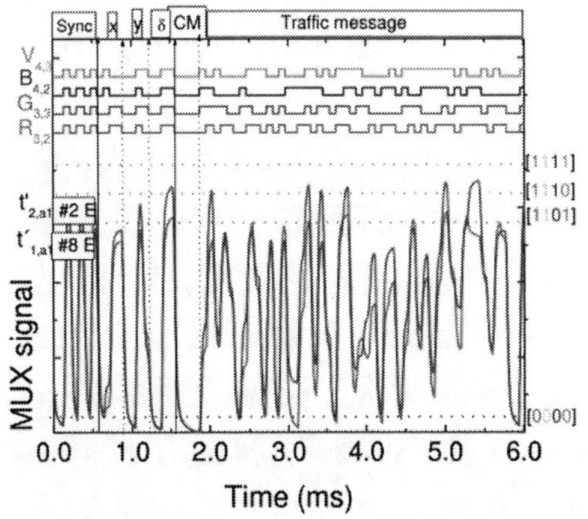

a)

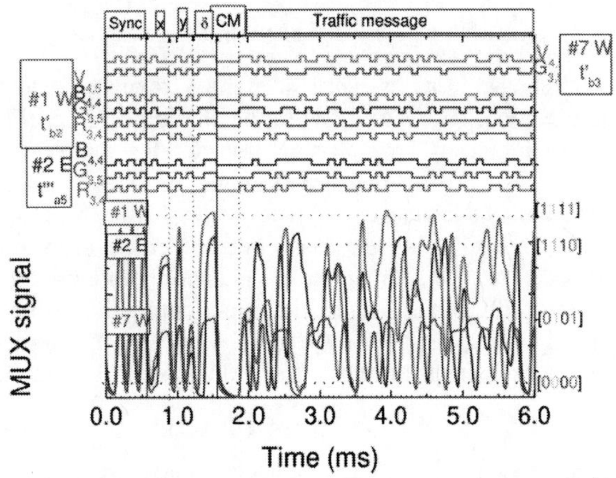

b)

Figure 9 Normalized MUX signal responses and the assigned decoded messages acquired by vehicles a_5, b_2, b_3 at different response times. a) Vehicle a_1, poses #8E and #2E. b) Vehicle a_5, pose #2E, and Vehicle b_2 poses #7W and, b_3 at #1W.

Figuring out Figures 3 and 6, Figure 9a shows the MUX signals assigned to response messages received by Vehicle a_1, driving the right lane, that enters Cell $C_{4,2}$ in #2 (t'_1, Phase1, green pose), goes straight to E to position #8 (t'_2, Phase1, green pose). Then, this vehicle enters the crossroad through #8 and leaves it in the exit #2 keeping always the same direction (E). In Figure 9b, vehicles b_2 and b_3 approach the intersection after having asking permission to cross. Upon the last follower vehicle a_5 leaving the intersection (end of Phase 2), they receive authorization. Then, Phase 3 begins with vehicle b_1 heading to the intersection (W) (pose red) while vehicles a_i ($1<i<5$) follows its destination towards E (pose green).

C. Traffic Signal Phasing

The traffic controller uses queue, request and response messages, from the a_i, b_i, c_i, e_i and f_i vehicles, fusing the self-localizations $q_i(t)$ with theirs space relative poses $q_{ij}(t)$ (dotted lines in Figure 7) to generate phase durations appropriate to accommodate the demand on each cycle.

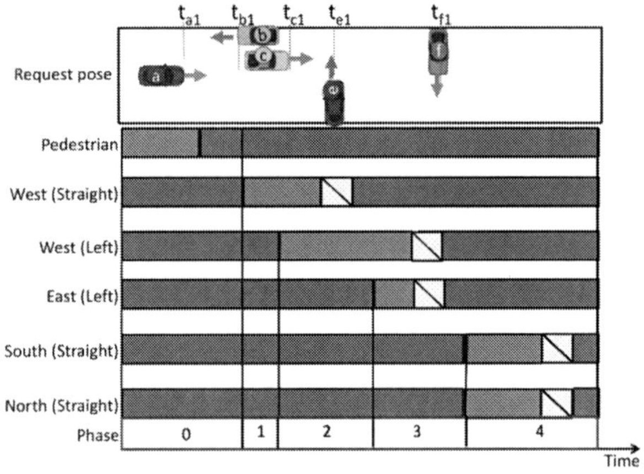

Figure 10 Requested phasing of traffic flows

Vehicle x is assigned a unique time to enter the intersection, $t[x]$. According to the phasing diagram (Figure 6), in Figure 10, the phasing flow for the intersection is visualized. From the capacity point of view it is more efficient, if Vehicle c_1 is given access before Vehicles b_i, and Vehicle c_2 is given access before Vehicle e, forming a west left turn of set of vehicles (platoon) before giving way to the fourth phase (north and south conflicting flows), as stated in Figure 8. The speed of Vehicle e was reduced, keeping a safe distance between Vehicle e and Vehicle d.

IV. CONCLUSIONS

Using V-VLC-ready connected cars, we propose a queue/request/response approach for managing four-legged intersections. A communication scenario is stablished and a "mesh/cellular" hybrid network configuration proposed. As a PoC, a phasing of traffic flows is suggested. In this study, the vehicles' arrival is controlled and they are scheduled to cross intersections at predetermined times to minimize traffic delays. V2I2V communication provides real-time data on queues, requests, and messages distances, including queue, request, and message travel times that influence traffic channeling in various routes. Delays between left-turns and forward movements are also allocated taking into account the pose analysis. Based on the simulated/experimental results, the proposed VLC cooperative architecture appears to be appropriate for the intended applications. The introduction of VLC between connected vehicles and the surrounding infrastructure allows the direct monitoring of critical points that are related to the queue formation and dissipation, relative speed thresholds and inter-vehicle spacing increasing the safety.

ACKNOWLEDGEMENTS

This work was sponsored by FCT – Fundação para a Ciência e a Tecnologia, within the Research Unit CTS – Center of Technology and Systems, reference UIDB/00066/2020.

REFERENCES

[1] D. Elliott,W. Keen, and L. Miao, "Recent advances in connected and automated vehicles" Journal of Traffic and Transportation Engineering, Vol. 6, Issue 2, pp.109-131, April 2019.

[2] N. Jitendra and Bajpai, "Emerging vehicle technologies & the search for urban mobility solutions,Urban, Planning and TransportResearch, 4:1, pp.83-100, DOI: 10.1080/21650020.2016.1185964, 2016.

[3] N. Wang, Y. Qiao, W. Wang, S. Tang, and J. Shen, "Visible Light Communication based Intelligent Traffic Light System: Designing and Implementation,"2018 Asia Communications and Photonics Conference (ACP) DOI: 10.1109/ACP.2018.8595791, 2018.

[4] N. Cheng, et al. "Big data driven vehicular networks," IEEE Network, vol. 32, no. 6, pp.160–167, Nov. 2018.

[5] H. Parth. X. Pathak, H. Pengfei, and M. Prasant,"Visible Light Communication, Networking and Sensing: Potential and Challenges," September 2015, IEEE Communications Surveys & Tutorials 17(4): Fourthquarter 2015, pp. 2047–2077, 2015.

[6] S. Caputo, et al. "Measurement-based VLC channel characterization for I2V communications in a real urban scenario," Veh. Commun., vol. 28, Apr. 2021, Art. no. 100305.

[7] P. Pribyl, M. Pribyl, Lom, and M. Svitek, "Modeling of smart cities based on ITS architecture," IEEE Intell. Transp. Syst. Mag., vol. 11, no. 4, pp. 28–36, Nov. 2019.

[8] R. Miucic, "Connected Vehicles: Intelligent Transportation Systems." Cham, Switzerland: Springer, 2019.

[9] M. A. Vieira, M. Vieira, P. Louro, and P. Vieira, "Bi-directional communication between infrastructures and vehicles through visible light," Proc. SPIE 11207, Fourth International Conference on Applications of Optics and Photonics, 112070C, 3 October 2019; doi: 10.1117/12.2526500. 2019.

[10] M. A. Vieira, M. Vieira, P., Vieira, and P. Louro, "Optical signal processing for a smart vehicle lighting system using a-SiCH technology," Proc. SPIE 10231, Optical Sensors 2017, 102311L, 2017.

[11] Y. Zhu, W. Liang, J. Zhang, and Y. Zhang, "Space-Collaborative Constellation Designs for MIMO Indoor Visible Light Communications," IEEE Photonics Technology Letters, vol. 27, no. 15, pp. 1667–1670, 2015.

[12] A. Yousefpour, et al., "All one needs to know about fog computing and related edge computing paradigms: A complete survey", Journal of Systems Architecture,Volume 98, pp. 289-330, 2019.

[13] M. A. Vieira; M. Vieira; P. Louro, and P. Vieira, "Cooperative vehicular communication systems based on visible light communication," Opt. Eng. 57(7), 076101 2018.

VLC Based Guidance System to Be Used by Mobile Users Inside Large Buildings.

Manuela Vieira, Manuel Augusto Vieira, Paula Louro, Alessandro Fantoni
ADETC/ISEL/IPL,
R. Conselheiro Emídio Navarro, 1959-007
Lisboa, Portugal
CTS-UNINOVA
Quinta da Torre, Monte da Caparica, 2829-516,
Caparica, Portugal

e-mail: mv@isel.ipl.pt, mv@isel.pt, plouro@deetc.isel.pt, afantoni@deetc.isel.ipl.pt

Pedro Vieira
ADETC/ISEL/IPL,
R. Conselheiro Emídio Navarro, 1959-007
Lisboa, Portugal
Instituto das Telecomunicações
Instituto Superior Técnico, 1049-001,
Lisboa, Portugal
e-mail: pvieira@isel.pt

Abstract— **The main goal of this paper is a Visible Light Communication (VLC) based guidance system to be used by mobile users inside large buildings. This system is composed of several transmitters (ceiling luminaries), which transmit map information and path guidance messages. Mobile devices, with VLC support, decode the information. A mesh cellular hybrid structure is proposed. The luminaires, via VLC, deliver their geographic position and specific information to the users, making them available for whatever use they request. The communication protocol, coding/decoding techniques, and error control are examined. Bidirectional communication is implemented and the best route to navigate through venue calculated. We propose several guidance services and multi-person cooperative localization. By analyzing the results, it became clear that the system not only provides self-location, but also the capability to determine the direction of travel and to interact with information received in order to optimize the route towards a static or dynamic destination.**

Keywords- Visible Light Communication; Assisted indoor navigation; Bidirectional Communication; Optical sensors; Transmitter/Receiver; Edge-Fog architecture.

I. INTRODUCTION

The main goal is to specify the system conceptual design and define a set of use cases for a VLC based guidance system to be used by mobile users inside large buildings. The most obvious method of using guidance signs is through billboards located in high traffic areas. Handheld devices allow customers to stay informed, gather information and communicate with others without being tied to a physical location.

With the rapid increase in wireless mobile devices, the continuous increase of wireless data traffic has brought challenges to the continuous reduction of radio frequency (RF) spectrum, which has also driven the demand for alternative technologies [1][2]. In order to solve the contradiction between the explosive growth of data and the consumption of spectrum resources, VLC has become the development direction of the next generation communication network with its huge spectrum resources, high security, low cost, and so on [3][4].

With the increasing shortage of radio frequency spectrum and the development of Light-Emitting Diodes (LEDs), VLC has attracted extensive attention. Compared to conventional wireless communications, VLC has higher rates, lower power consumption, and less electromagnetic interferences. VLC is a data transmission technology that can easily be employed in indoor environments since it can use the existing LED lighting infrastructure with simple modifications [5] [6]. The use of white polychromatic LEDs offers the possibility of Wavelength Division Multiplexing (WDM), which enhances the transmission data rate. A WDM receiver based on tandem a-SiC:H/a-Si:H pin/pin light controlled filter can be used [7] [8] to decode the received information. Here, when different visible signals are encoded in the same optical transmission path, the device multiplexes the different optical channels, performs different filtering processes (amplification, switching, and wavelength conversion) and finally decodes the encoded signals recovering the transmitted information.

Visible light can be used as an Identifier (ID) system and can be employed for identifying the building itself. The main idea is to divide the service area into spatial beams originating from the different ID light sources and identify each beam with a unique timed sequence of light signals. The signboards, based on arrays of LEDs, positioned in strategic directions [9], are modulated acting as down- and up-link channels in the bidirectional communication. For the consumer services, the applications are enormous. Positioning, navigation, security and even mission critical services are possible use cases that should be implemented.

In this paper, a VLC based guidance system to be used by mobile users inside large buildings is proposed. After the Introduction, in Section II, a model for the system is proposed and the communication system described. In Section III, the main experimental results are presented, downlink and uplink transmission is implemented and the best route to navigate calculated. In Section IV, the conclusions are drawn.

II. SYSTEM MODEL

The system model of the proposed system will be presented in this section.

A. *Communication system*

The system model is composed by two modules: the transmitter and the receiver. The block diagram is presented in Figure 1. Both communication modules are software defined, where modulation/demodulation can be programed.

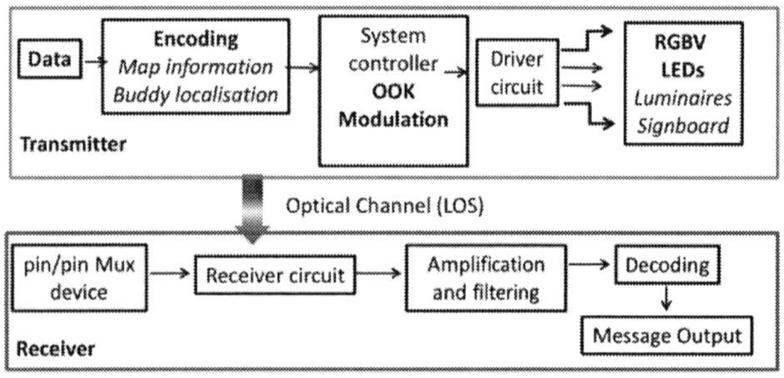

Figure 1. Block diagram. System model of the proposed control scheme applied to OOK modulation.

Data from the sender is converted into an intermediate data representation, byte format, and converted into light signals emitted by the transmitter module. The data bit stream is input to a modulator where an ON–OFF Keying (OOK) modulation is utilized. On the transmission side, a modulation and conversion from digital to analog data is done. The driver circuit will keep an average value (DC power level) for illumination, combining it with the analog data intended for communication. The visible light emitted by the LEDs passes through the transmission medium and is then received by the MUX device.

To realize both the communication and the building illumination, white light tetra-chromatic sources (WLEDs) are used providing a different data channel for each chip. The transmitter and receiver relative positions are displayed in Figure 2a. Each luminaire is composed of four polichromatic WLEDs framed at the corners of a square. At each node, only one chip is modulated for data transmission (see Figure 2b), the Red (R: 626 nm, 25 $\mu W/cm^2$), the Green (G: 530 nm, 46 $\mu W/cm^2$), the Blue (B: 470 nm, 60 $\mu W/cm^2$) or the Violet (V, 400 nm, 150 $\mu W/cm^2$). Data is encoded, modulated and converted into light signals emitted by the transmitters. Modulation and digital-to-analog conversion of the information bits is done using signal processing techniques. An OOK modulation scheme was used to code the information. This way digital data is represented by the presence or absence of a carrier wave.

The signal is propagating through the optical channel, and a VLC receiver, at the reception end of the communication link, is responsible to extract the data from the modulated light beam. It transforms the light signal into an electrical signal that is subsequently decoded to extract the transmitted information. The obtained voltage is then processed, by using signal conditioning techniques (adaptive bandpass filtering and amplification, triggering and demultiplexing), until the data signal is reconstructed at the data processing unit (digital conversion, decoding and decision) [10] [11]. At last, the message will be output to the users.

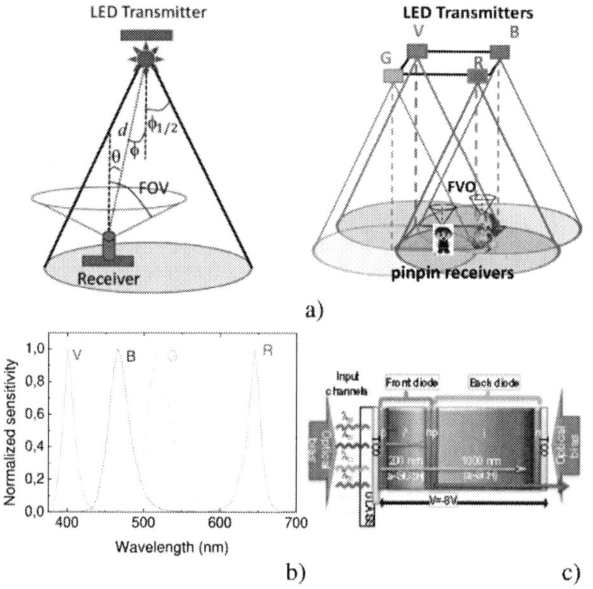

Figure 2. a)3D relative positions of the transmitters and receivers. b) Spectra of the input channels. c)Configuration and operation of the pin/pin Mux device

On the receiving side, a MUX photodetector acts as an active filter for the visible region of the light spectrum. The integrated filter consists of a p-i'(a-SiC:H)-n/p-i(a-Si:H)-n heterostructure with low conductivity doped layers [7] as displayed in Figure 2c. Independent tuning of each channel is performed by steady state violet optical bias (λ_{bias}= 2300 $\mu W/cm^2$) superimposed from the front side of the device and the generated photocurrent measured at -8V. The generated photocurrent is processed using a transimpedance circuit obtaining a proportional voltage. Since the photodetector response is insensitive to the frequency, phase, or polarization of the carriers, this kind of receiver is useful for intensity-modulated signals. After receiving the signal, it is in turn filtered, amplified, and converted back to digital format for demodulation. The system controller consists of a set of programmable modules.

In this system model, there are a few assumptions that should be noted: The channel state information is available both at the receiver and the transmitter; compared with the direct light, the reflected light is much weaker in the indoor VLC systems; only the Line OF Sight (LOS) path is considered and the multipath influence is not considered in the proposed indoor VLC system.

The received channel can be expresssed as:

$$y=\mu hx+n \quad (1)$$

where y represents the received signal, x the transmitted signal, μ is the photoelectric conversion factor which can be normalized as $\mu = 1$, h is the channel gain and n is the additive white Gaussian noise of which the mean is 0.

The LEDs are modeled as Lambertian sources where the luminance is distributed uniformly in all directions, whereas the luminous intensity is different in all directions. The luminous intensity for a Lambertian source is given by Equation (2) [12]:

$$I(\emptyset)=I_N \cos(\emptyset)^m \quad ; \quad m=\frac{\ln(2)}{\ln(\cos(\phi_{1/2}))} \quad (2)$$

I_N is the maximum luminous intensity in the axial direction, ϕ is the angle of irradiance and m is the order derived from a Lambertian pattern. For the proposed system, the commercial white LEDs were designed for illumination purposes, exhibiting a wide half intensity angle ($\phi_{1/2}$) of 60º. Thus, the Lambertian order m is 1. Friis' transmission equation is frequently used to calculate the maximum range by which a wireless link can operate. The coverage map is obtained by calculating the link budget from the Friis transmission equation [13].

The Friis transmission equation relates the received power (P_R) to the transmitted power (P_E), path loss distance (L_R), and gains from the emitter (G_E) and receiver (G_R) in a free-space communication link.

$$P_{R\,[dBm]}=P_{E\,[dBm]}+G_{E\,[dB]}+G_{R\,[dB]}-L_{R\,[dB]} \quad (3)$$

Taking into account Figure 2a, the path loss distance and the emitter gain will be given by:

$$L_{R\,[dB]}=22+20\ln\frac{d}{\lambda} \quad (4)$$

$$G_{E\,[dB]}=\frac{(m+1)A}{2\pi d_{E-R}^2} I(\emptyset)\cos(\theta) \quad (5)$$

With A de area of the photodetector and d_{E_R} the distance between each transmitter and every point on the receiver plane. Due to their filtering properties of the receptors the gains are strongly dependent on the wavelength of the pulsed LEDs. Gains (G_R) of 5, 4, 1.7 and 0.8 were used, respectively, for the R, G, B and V LEDs. I_N of 730 mcd, 650 mcd, 800 mcd and 900 mcd were considered. The coverage map, for a square unit cell, (see Figure 5).

B. Building model and Architecture

Lighting in large environments is designed to illuminate the entire space in a uniform way. The proposed scenario is a multi-level building. Ceiling plans for the LED array layout, in floor level is shown in Figure 3. A square lattice topology was considered for each level.

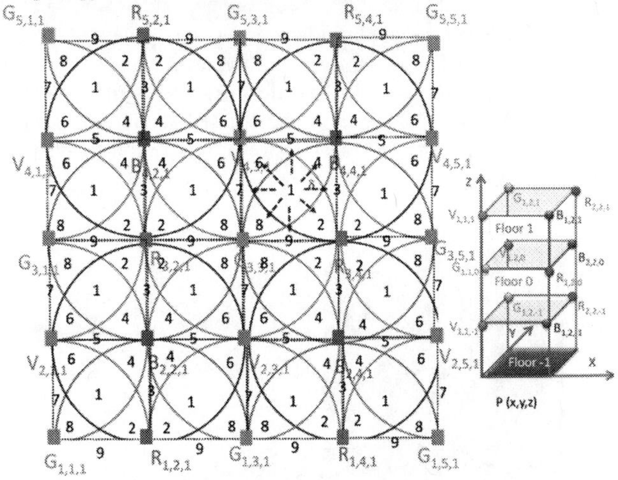

Figure 3. Clusters of cells in square topology. Illustration of the optical scenario. (RGBV =modulated LEDs spots).

In fog /edge computing, computing, storage, networking, and data management services are provided on nodes within close proximity to IoT devices, bridging the gap between the cloud and end devices. In Figure 4, the proposed architecture is illustrated. Under this architecture, the short-range mesh network purpose is twofold: enable edge computing and device-to-cloud communication, by ensuring a secure communication from a luminaire controller to the edge computer or datacenter (I2CM), through a neighbor luminaire/signboard controller with an active cellular connection; and enable peer-to-peer communication (I2I), to exchange information.

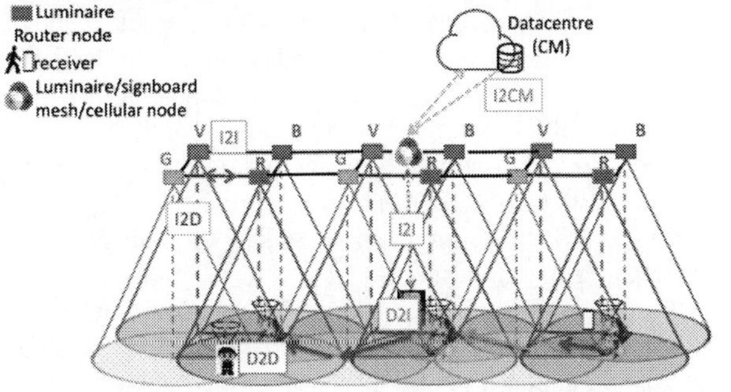

Figure 4. Mesh and cellular hybrid architecture.

A user navigates from outdoor to indoor. It sends a request message (D2I) to find the right track and, in the available time, he adds customized points of interest (guidance services). The requested information (I2D) is sent by the emitters at the ceiling to its receiver.

In this architecture, the polychromatic WLEDs are placed on the ceiling in a square lattice topology (see Figure 3), but only one, chip is modulated (R, G, B, V). The principle is that each WLED transmits a VLC signal with a unique identifier. The optical receiver uses this information and a position algorithm, based on the received joint transmission, calculates the track of the user.

To receive the I2D information from several transmitters, the receiver must be located at the overlap of the circles that set the transmission range (radial) of each transmitter.

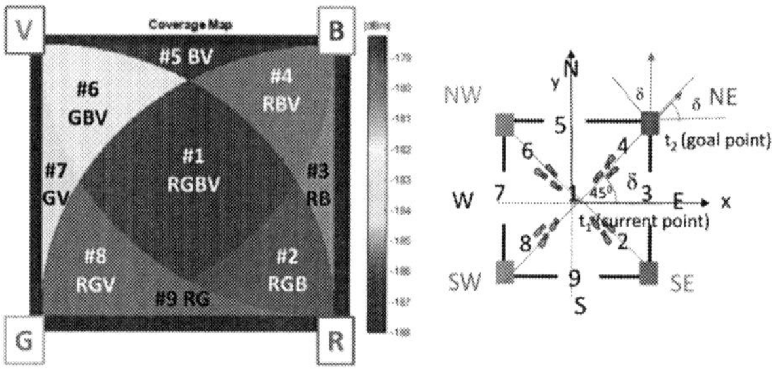

Figure 5. Illustration of the coverage map in the unit cell: footprint regions (#1-#9) and steering angle codes (2-9).

Taking into account (1)-(5), the coverage map for a square unit cell is displayed in Figure 5. All the values were converted to decibel (dB).The nine possible overlaps (#1-#9), defined as fingerprint regions, as well as receiver orientations (2-9 steering angles; δ) are also pointed out for the unit square cell, in Figure 5. The input of the aided navigation system is the coded signal sent by the transmitters to an identify user (I2D), and includes its position in the network *P(x, y, z)*, inside the unit cell and the steering angle, δ, that guides the user across his path at a given time, *t*. The device receives multiple signals, finds the centroid of the received coordinates, and stores it as the reference point position. Nine reference points, for each unit cell, are identified giving a fine-grained resolution in the localization of the mobile device across each cell.

The indoor route throughout the building (track; *q(x, y, z, δ, t)*) is presented to the user by a responding message (I2D) transmitted by the ceiling luminaires that work also either as router or mesh/cellular nodes.

Two-way communication (D2I-I2D) between users and the infrastructure is carried out through a neighbor luminaire/signboard controller with an active cellular connection (I2CM). With this request/response concept, the generated landmark-based instructions help the user to unambiguously identify the correct decision point where a change of direction (pose) is needed, as well as offer information for the user to confirm that he/she is on the right way.

C. *Communication protocol, coding/decoding techniques and error control*

To code the information, an On-Off Keying (OOK) modulation scheme was used and it was considered a synchronous transmission based on a 64- bits data frame. The coded transmitted signals are shown in Figure 6 along with their respective MUX signals.

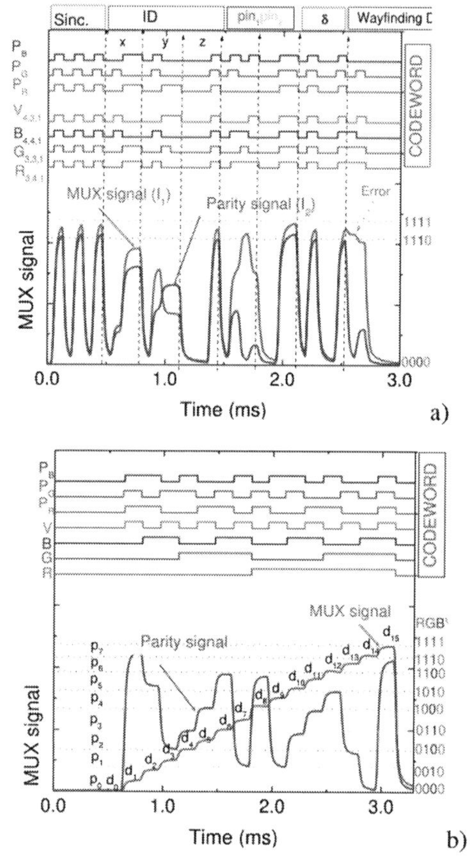

Figure 6. Code and parity MUX/DEMUX signals. On the top the transmitted channels [R G B V : P_R P_G P_B] are shown. a) Calibrated cell. b) Error control assigned to a request from user "7261" at $C_{4,3,1}$; #1 N.

All messages, in a frame, start with the header labelled as Sync, a block of 5 bits. The same synchronization header [10101], in an ON-OFF pattern, is imposed simultaneously to all emitters. The next block (ID) gives the geolocation (*x, y, z* coordinates) of the emitters inside the array ($X_{i,j,k}$). Cell's IDs are encoded using a 4 bits binary representation for the decimal number. So, the next 12 (4+4+4) bits in are assigned, respectively, to the *x*, *y* and *z* coordinates (*i, j, k*) of the emitter in the array. If the message is diffused by the CM transmitter, a pattern [0000] precedes this identification. When bidirectional communication is required, the user has to register by choosing a user name (pin_1) with 4 decimal numbers, each one associated to a color channel. So, to compose the decimal code each digit (0-9) has its own color, codified in a 4-binary bit code. Whenever buddy friend services are required, the 4-binary code of the meeting (pin_2) must be entered. In a frame time, The δ block (steering angle (δ)) completes the pose, $q(x, y, \delta, t)$. Eight steering angles along the cardinal points and coded with the same number of the footprints in the unit cell (Figure 5) are possible from a start point to the next goal. The codes assigned to the pin_2 and to δ are the same in all the channels. In the absence of wayfinding services these last three blocks are set to zero and the user receives only its own location. The last block is used to transmit the wayfinding message. A stop bit is used at the end of each frame.

Using the photocurrent signal measured by the photodetector, it is necessary to decode the received information. A calibration curve is previously defined to establish this assignment [14]. As displayed in Figure 6b, calibration curves make use of 16 distinct photocurrent thresholds which correspond to a bit sequence that allows all the sixteen combinations of the four RGBV input channels (2^4). If the calibrated levels (d_0-d_{15}) are compared to the different four-digit binary codes assigned to each level, then the decoding is obvious, and the message may be read [14]. Due to the proximity of successive levels (see Figure 6a) occasional errors occur in the decoded information. A parity check is performed after the word has been read [15]. The parity bits are the SUM bits of the three-bit additions of violet pulsed signal with two additional RGB bits and defined as:

$$P_R = V \oplus R \oplus B; \; P_G = V \oplus R \oplus G; \; P_B = V \oplus G \oplus B \quad (6)$$

In Figure 6b, the MUX signal that arises from the transmission of the four calibrated RGBV wavelength channels and the MUX signal that results from the generation of the synchronized parity MUX are displayed. On the top the seven bit word [R,G,B,V, P_R, P_G, P_B] of the transmitted inputs guides the eyes. The colours red, green, blue and violet were assigned respectively to P_R, P_G , P_B and P_V. For simplicity the received data ($d_{0\text{-}15}$ levels) is marked in the correspondent MUX slots as well as the parity levels marked as horizontal lines. On the top the decoded 7-bit coded word is exhibited. In the right side 4-bit binary codes assigned to the eight parity sublevels are inserted.

In Figure 6a we illustrate how error control is achieved using check parity bits. A request from user "7261" is shown at $C_{4,3,1}$; #1 N, along with the matching parity signal. Results show that without check parity bits, decoding was difficult primarily when levels were close together (dotted arrow). Based on the results for the analysed cases, the BER is high (4.6% without error correction) whereas it is negligible with error correction.

III. MULTI-PERSON COOPERATIVE LOCALIZATION AND GUIDANCE SERVICES

Via the control manager, a handheld device with VLC connectivity communicates bidirectionally with a signboard receiver in each unit cell (#1). Each user (D2I) uplinks to the local controller a "request" message with the pose, $q_i(t)$, (x, y, z, δ), user code (pin_1) and also adds its needs (code meeting and wayfinding data). For route coordination the CM, using the information of the network's VLC location capability, downlinks a personalized "response" message to each client at the requested pose with his wayfinding needs (I2D).

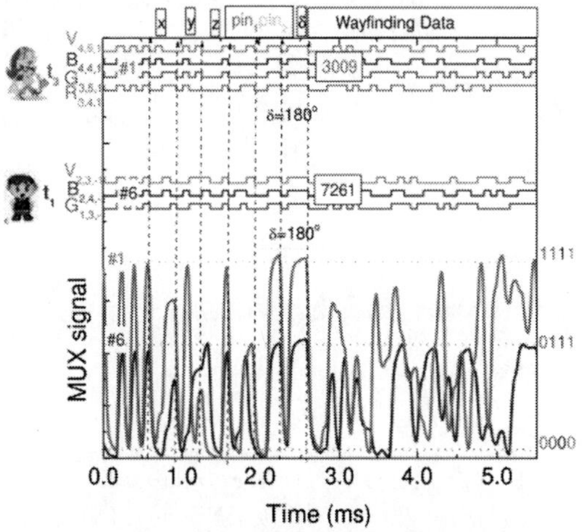

Figure 7. MUX/DEMUX signals assigned requests from two users ("3009" and "7261") at different poses ($C_{4,4,,1}$; #1W and $C_{2,3,-1}$; #6 W) and in successive instants (t_1 and t_3).

In Figure 7, the MUX synchronized signals received by two users that have requested guidance services, at different times, are displayed. We have assumed that a user located at $C_{2,3,-1}$, arrived first (t_1), auto-identified as ("7261") and informed the controller of his intention to find a friend for a previously scheduled meeting (code 3). A buddy list is then generated and will include all the users who have the same meeting code. User "3009" arrives later (t_3), sends the alert notification ($C_{4,4,1}$; t_3) to be triggered when his friend is in his floor vicinity, level 1, identifies himself ("3009") and uses the same code (code 3), to track the best way to his meeting.

Upon receiving this request (t_3), the buddy finder service uses the location information from both devices to determine the proximity of their owners ($q_{ij}(t)$) and provides the best route to the meeting, avoiding crowded areas.

The pedestrian movement along the path can be thought as a queue, where the pedestrians arrive at a path, wait if the path is congested and then move once the congestion reduces. In Figure 7, a graphical representation of the simultaneous localization and mapping problem using connectivity as a function of node density, mobility and transmission range is illustrated.

The following parameters are therefore needed to model the queuing system: The initial arrival time (t_0) and the path, defined as the time when the pedestrian leaves the previous path and the actual movement along the path, $q_i(t, t')$. Here, the service time is calculated using walking speed and distance of the path. The number of service units or resources is determined by the capacity of the pathway, $n(q_i (x,y,z, \delta, t))$ and walking speed which depends on the number of request services, and on the direction of movement along the pathway $q_i (x,y,z, \delta, t)$. The pedestrians are served as soon as the request message is appended by the CM (response message) as displayed in Figure 8.

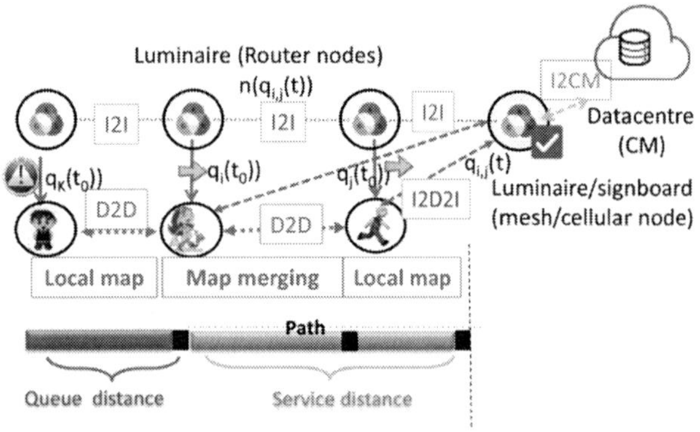

Figure 8 Graphical representation of the simultaneous localization and mapping problem using connectivity as a function of node density, mobility and transmission range.

If the number of pedestrians exceeds the path capacity, a backlog is automatically formed until the starting node. The hybrid controller integrates the number of requests and individual positions received during the same time interval. Once the individual positions are known, $q_i (t)$, the relative positions are calculated, $q_{ij} (t)$. If the relative position is less than a threshold distance, a crowded region locally exists, and an alert message is sent for the users. This alert allows the CM to recalculate, in real time, the best route for the users, $q_i (t,t')$, that request wayfinding services avoiding crowded regions.

IV. CONCLUSIONS

A VLC based guidance system to be used by mobile users inside large buildings was proposed and characterized. According to global results, the location of a mobile receiver is found in conjunction with data transmission. VLC's dynamic LED-aided guidance system is designed to give users accurate route guidance and enable navigation and geotracking. The multi-person cooperative localization system detects crowded regions and alerts the user to reschedule meetups, as well as provides guidance information. With those alerts, the CM can recalculate, in real time, the best route for users requesting wayfinding services, avoiding crowded areas.

ACKNOWLEDGEMENTS

This work was sponsored by FCT – Fundação para a Ciência e a Tecnologia, within the Research Unit CTS – Center of Technology and Systems, reference UIDB/00066/2020.

REFERENCES

[1] F. Zafar, D. Karunatilaka, and R. Parthiban, " Dimming Schemes for Visible Light Communication: The State of Research. IEEE Wireless Commun., 22, pp. 29–35, 2015,.

[2] L. U. Khan, "Visible Light Communication: Applications, Architecture, Standardization and Research Challenges," Digit. Commun. Netw. 3, pp. 78–88, 2017.

[3] N. U. Hassan, A. Naeem, M. A. Pasha, T. Jadoon, and C. Yuen, "Indoor positioning using visible led lights: A survey,"ACM Comput. Surv., vol. 48, pp.1–32, 2015.

[4] E. Ozgur, E. Dinc, and O. B. Akan, "Communicate to illuminate: State-of-the-art and research challenges for visible light communications," Physical Communication 17, pp. 72–85, 2015.

[5] D. Tsonev, et al., "A 3-Gb/s single-LED OFDM-based wireless VLC link using a Gallium Nitride μLED," IEEE Photon. Technol. Lett. 26 (7), pp. 637–640, 2014.

[6] D. O'Brien, et al., "Indoor visible light communications: challenges and prospects," Proc. SPIE 7091, 709106, 2008.

[7] M. Vieira, P. Louro, M. Fernandes, M. A. Vieira, A. Fantoni and J. Costa "Three Transducers Embedded into One Single SiC Photodetector: LSP Direct Image Sensor, Optical Amplifier and Demux Device," Advances in Photodiodes InTech, Chap.19, pp. 403-425, 2011.

[8] M. A. Vieira, P. Louro, M. Vieira, A. Fantoni, and A. Steiger-Garção, "Light-activated amplification in Si-C tandem devices: A capacitive active filter model," IEEE sensor journal, 12, NO. 6, pp. 1755-1762, 2012.

[9] S. B. Park, et al., "Information broadcasting system based on visible light signboard," presented at Wireless and Optical Communication 2007, Montreal, Canada, 2007.

[10] M. Vieira, M. A. Vieira., P. Louro., P. Vieira, A. Fantoni, "Light-emitting diodes aided indoor localization using visible light communication technology," Opt. Eng. 57(8), 087105, 2018.

[11] M. A. Vieira, M. Vieira, P. Louro, and P. Vieira, "Bi-directional communication between infrastructures and vehicles through visible light," Proc. SPIE 11207, Fourth International Conference on Applications of Optics and Photonics, 112070C (3 October 2019); doi: 10.1117/12.2526500. 2019.

[12] Zhu, Y., Liang, W., Zhang, J., and Zhang, Y., "Space-Collaborative Constellation Designs for MIMO Indoor Visible Light Communications," IEEE Photonics Technology Letters, vol. 27, no. 15, pp. 1667–1670, 2015.

[13] H. T. Friis "A note on a simple transmission formula" Proc. IRE34, pp. 254–256, 1946.

[14] M. Vieira, M. A. Vieira, P. Louro, A. Fantoni, P. Vieira, "Dynamic VLC navigation system in Crowded Buildings", International Journal On Advances in Software, v 14 n 3&4, pp. 141-150, 2021.

[15] M. A. Vieira, M. A., Vieira, M., Silva, V., Louro, P., Costa, J., "Optical signal processing for data error detection and correction using a-SiCH technology," Phys. Status Solidi C 12 (12), 1393–1400 (2015).

Impact of the Packaging on the Static Behavior of Piezoresitive Pressure Sensor Dedicated to the Monitoring of Blast Waves

Bilel Achour, Lilian Marty, Kevin Sanchez, Samuel Charlot, Xavier Dollat, Benjamin Reig, Laurent Bouscayrol, Aurélie Lecestre, Anthony Coustou, André Ferrand, Hervé Aubert, Patrick Pons
CNRS-LAAS, Toulouse University
Toulouse, France

E-mails: bachour@laas.fr, lmarty@laas.fr, ksanchezba@laas.fr, scharlot@laas.fr, xavier.dollat@laas.fr, breig@laas.fr, laurent.bouscayrol@laas.fr, alecestre@laas.fr, acoustou@laas.fr, andre.ferrand@insa-toulouse.fr, aubert@laas.fr, ppons@laas.fr

Abstract— **The packaging is an important step, allowing to transform the transducer chip into a sensor. This step is necessary to perform the sensor characterization in a real environment, while minimizing the impact of the influence parameters on the sensor response. This study concerns the impact of the packaging on the static response of a miniature pressure sensor dedicated to the monitoring of blast waves. The transducer is based on 5 µm - thick rectangular (55 µm x 135 µm) silicon membrane and piezoresistive gauges. Pressure sensitivity measurements are performed using stressed and non-stressed sensor's holder configurations. Measurements results indicate that the pressure sensitivity is doubled when the sensor's holder is stressed. Finite Element Method simulations using COMSOL Multiphysics software show here that this result originates from the deformation of the sensor's holder, which leads to the deflection of the thin silicon membrane.**

Keywords – blast waves; pressure sensor; packaging; mechanical stress; Finite Element Method.

I. INTRODUCTION

Shock waves are characterized by the propagation of a pressure discontinuity at supersonic speeds, which makes difficult the measurement of the overpressure peak [1]. For near-field experiments, the sensor's bandwidth required to ensure the accurate measurement of the overpressure is higher than 1 MHz [2]. To achieve such large bandwidths, the fundamental mechanical resonant frequency of pressure sensors must be far above 1 MHz (typically > 10 MHz).

However, the fundamental mechanical resonant frequency does not exceed a few MHz for commercial sensors dedicated to the monitoring of shock waves. To achieve higher mechanical resonant frequencies, studies focused on the design and fabrication of sensors using silicon or silicon dioxide micro-membranes with a lateral dimension of less than 100 µm and a thickness of a few microns [3]-[6]. However, the significant reduction of the membrane dimensions results in a very low sensitivity of the membrane deflection to applied pressure (typically, a few nm/bar). The measurement of such very small deflections is possible either from optical transduction [3]-[5], or by using strain gauges [6]. But the pressure sensor can be subjected to the deformation of its packaging, especially during dynamic characterizations [7]. Studies on high-bandwidth pressure sensors, published in open scientific Literature, generally do not address the impact of such deformation on sensor performances, whereas the experimental characterization of the sensors shows instabilities on the sensor's response after the passage of the shock wave front [3]-[6].

The work reported here aims to understand the impact of the packaging on the static response of piezoresistive pressure sensors dedicated to the monitoring of aerial shock waves. The obtained results will help us for the future design of optimized packaging dedicated to dynamic characterization of such sensors.

The paper is organised as follows. Section II is dedicated to the description of the pressure sensor, and Section III presents the experimental setup used for the static characterisation of the sensors. Measurement results are reported and analysed in Section IV. Mechanical simulation results are presented and discussed in Section V. Finally, the conclusion and perspectives of this work are drawn in Section VI.

II. PRESSURE SENSOR DESCRIPTION

The sensor is based on a rectangular silicon micro-membrane with 4 gauges located near its centre and connected in a Wheatstone bridge configuration (Figure 1). The manufacturing process of the sensor is detailed in [7]. The only difference with the design reported in [7] is the use of a Silicon-On-Insulator (SOI) substrate with 1 µm - thick buried silicon dioxide instead of a thickness of 2 µm. The main changes in the design relate to (see Figure 2): (a) lower access resistances to the Wheatstone bridge by defining the gauge length (P_+) by the distance between the heavily doped areas (P_{++}), (b) larger gauge size (2 µm × 10 µm instead of 1 µm × 5 µm) in order to reduce the impact of technological inaccuracies in the fabrication process, and finally (c) larger lateral dimensions of the membrane (55 µm × 135 µm instead of 40 µm × 100 µm) to compensate for larger gauge.

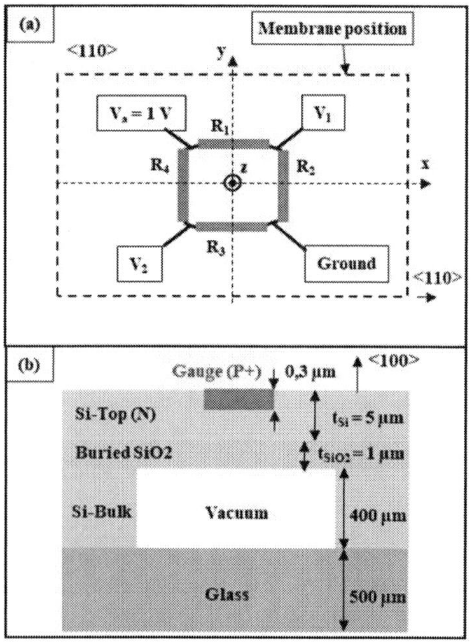

Figure 1. (a) Top view of the Wheatstone bridge reported on the membrane surface, (b) Cross sectional view of the transducer.

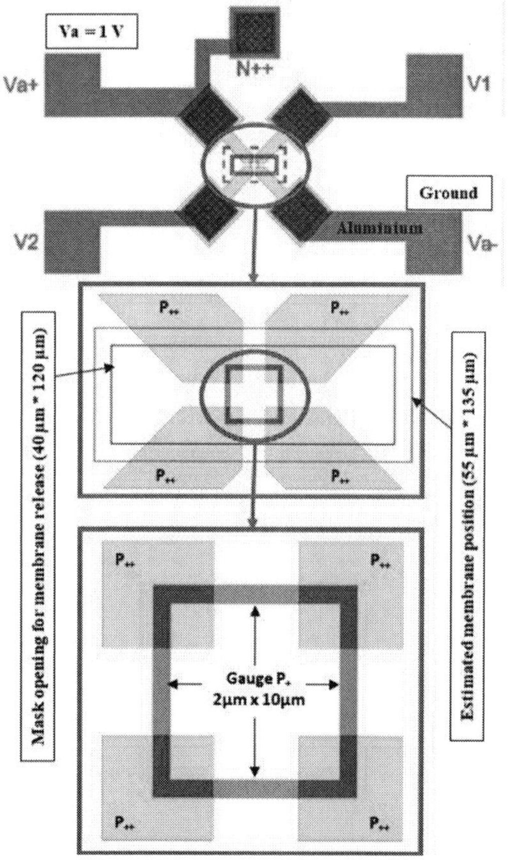

Figure 2. Top view of the mask used for the technological fabrication process (Purple / Green: Al / P_{++} interconnection, Orange: P_+ Gauge)

The theoretical fundamental mechanical resonant frequency F_0 of the membrane is about 10 MHz, that is, twice as low as the frequency reported in [7] but about 10 times higher than the fundamental resonant frequency of commercial sensors.

III. Experimental Set-Up for the Static Pressure Calibration

The setup used for the static calibration of pressure sensors is shown in Figure 3. The 4 mm - square silicon chip is glued on a 2.4 mm - thick stainless-steel holder using the thermosetting epoxy (Epotek-H70E) that is annealed for 90 minutes at 80°C. The device is then inserted into an airtight Static Pressure Box (SPB) connected to a pressure regulator (MENSOR APC600), which delivers a controlled relative pressure P_r ($P_r = P_{absolute} - P_{atmosphere}$). The pressure stability after regulation is ± 1 mbar. The sensor power supply (V_a = 960 mV ± 5 mV) is provided by the ELC- AL991S voltage generator. The differential output voltage V_s ($V_s = V_2 - V_1$) of the sensor is measured by using the Keithley-2000 multimeter with a resolution of 0.1 µV.

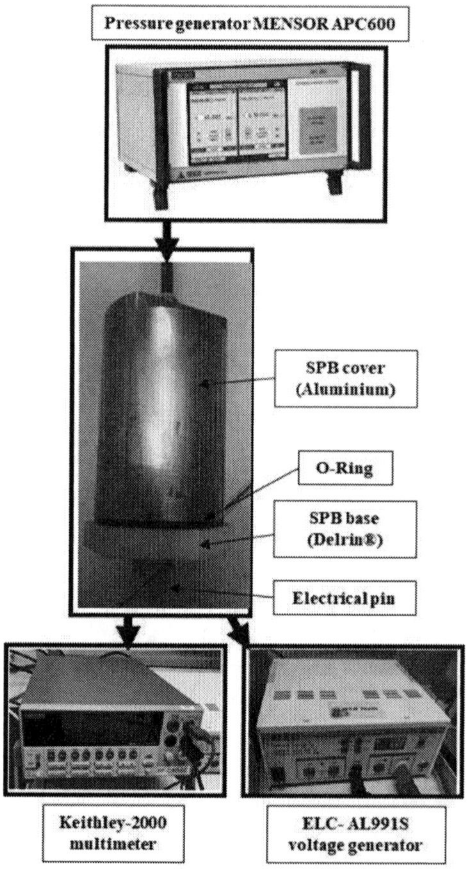

Figure 3. Experimental setup for the static pressure calibration of the sensor. (SPB: Sensor Pressure Box)

Two configurations are considered here to characterize the sensor:

i. Configuration *#S*: the sensor's holder is screwed onto the polymer (Derlin®) SPB base (Figure 4). The airtightness of the SPB is ensured by an O-ring (thickness ϕ_R = 2370 µm) embedded in the 1860 µm - depth groove. Before tightening process, the height of the O-ring protruding from the groove is therefore of 510 µm. The tightening of the screws is controlled by means of a 100 µm - thick calibrated metal wedge. The crushing of the O-ring is thus $\Delta\phi_R \cong 410$ µm (i.e. 17% of the initial thickness).

ii. Configuration *#F*: the sensor's holder is separated from the SPB base in order to reduce the stresses transferred to the sensor's holder (Figure 5). The airtightness of the SPB is then ensured by a holder without sensor, whose tightening is not controlled. The electrical connection between the two holders is achieved by using wires of about 5 cm long (the upper end is fitted with a female pin).

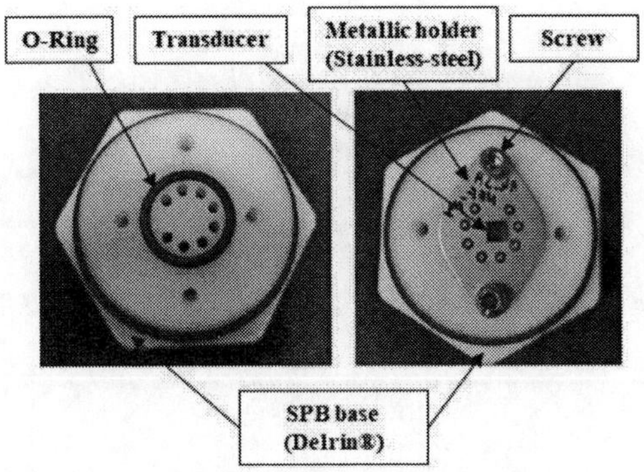

Figure 4. Configuration #S for the characterization of the sensor. (SPB: Sensor Pressure Box)

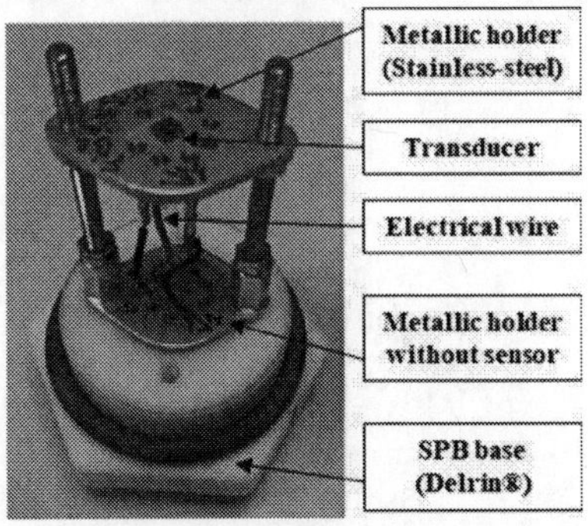

Figure 5. Configuration *#F* for the characterization of the sensor. (SPB: Sensor Pressure Box)

For both configurations *#S and #F*, the sensor pressure calibration is performed after a stabilisation phase, which takes at least 3 hours after the sensor placement inside the SPB. This phase is performed at atmospheric pressure and allows the mechanical relaxation of the sensor due to the stresses generated in holder. Next, the measurement of the voltage V_s is performed with increasing pressures, from the atmospheric pressure P_{atm} to a relative pressure P_r of 5 bar, with a step of 1 bar. The voltage V_s is measured about 2 minutes after the pressure stabilisation phase in order to achieve a good stability on V_s (± 10 µV). The voltage measurement for decreasing pressure is performed a few minutes after the first phase for which the pressure increases.

IV. MEASUREMENT OF THE SENSOR RESPONSE TO A STATIC PRESSURE

In Figure 6 to Figure 8 and Table I are displayed the measurement results for the two configurations (*#S* and *#F*) defined in Section III.

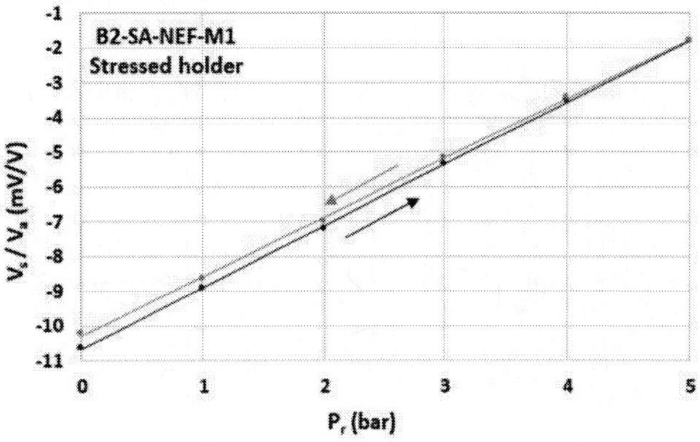

Figure 6. Sensor response in the configuration *#S* (Stressed holder).

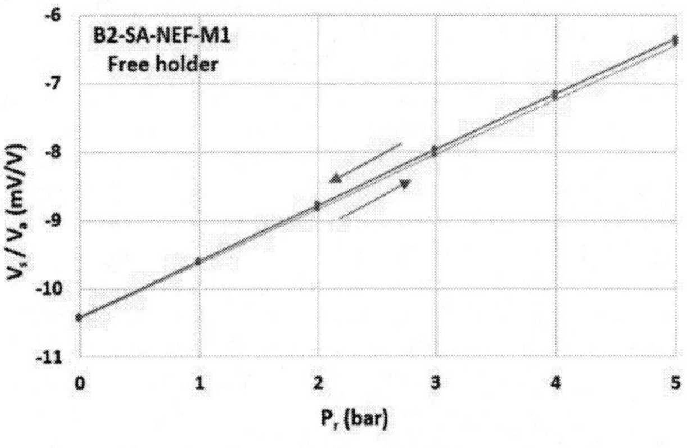

Figure 7. Sensor response in configuration *#F* (Holder without stress).

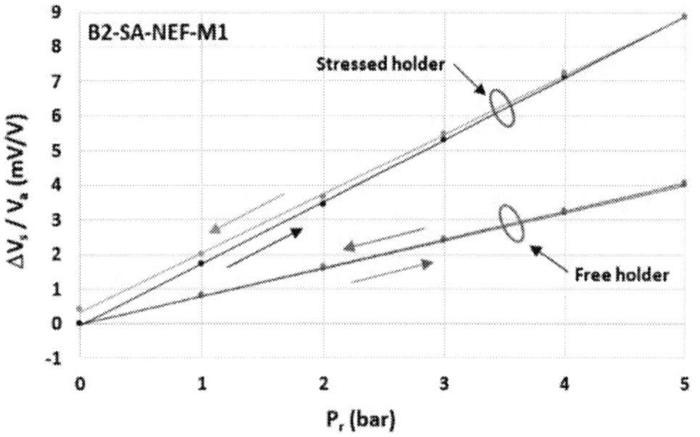

Figure 8. Comparison of the sensor responses in both configurations. The voltage variation ΔV_s is normalized by the voltage V_s obtained before applying the increasing pressure.

TABLE I. CHARACTERISITICS OF THE SENSOR RESPONSES

	Configuration #S (Stressed holder)	**Configuration #F (Free holder)**
Offset (Before applying the increasing pressure)	- 10.65 mV/V	- 10.42 mV/V
Offset (After applying the decreasing pressure)	- 10.21 mV/V	- 10.43 mV/V
Pressure sensitivity S_p (Increasing pressure)	1782 μV/V/bar	799 μV/V/bar
Pressure sensitivity S_p (Decreasing pressure)	1703 μV/V/bar	816 μV/V/bar

When the sensor's holder is not constrained (configuration *#F*), the magnitude of the pressure hysteresis is lower than the measurement accuracy (< 10 μV/V) and the pressure sensitivity S_p is between 799 μV/V/bar (for increasing pressure) and 816 μV/V/bar (for decreasing pressure). When the sensor's holder is constrained (configuration *#S*), the measurement results are less repeatable with a magnitude of the pressure hysteresis of 440 μV/V and a pressure sensitivity S_p ranging from 1782 μV/V/bar (for increasing pressure) to 1703 μV/V/bar (for decreasing pressure). This lower repeatability is probably related to partial stress relaxation in the sensor's holder during the pressure cycle. The stresses in the sensor's holder modify significantly the pressure sensitivity of the sensor (by a factor higher than 2).

V. SIMULATION OF THE SENSOR RESPONSE TO A STATIC PRESSURE

In order to identify the origin of the large increase of the sensor's pressure sensitivity when the holder is constrained, mechanical simulations are performed by using COMSOL Multiphysics software (Finite Element Method) (Figure 9 and Figure 10). The 4 mm - square Silicon-Glass sensor chip described in Figure 1 is connected to the elliptical-shaped metallic holder with a 100 μm - thick glue (Young's modulus 8 GPa). We assume that the center of the metallic holder and membrane coincide and that the axis of the screws is along the membrane length. The O-ring (in blue in Figure 10) is modelled as a spring whose mechanical stiffness K_S is estimated at 174 N/mm from the measurement of the O-ring crushing (between 30 μm and 270 μm) for a given mass. The tightening force F_T of the screw is modelled by a force applied along the edge (in green in Figure 10) and is adjusted to obtain the desired crushing of the O-ring.

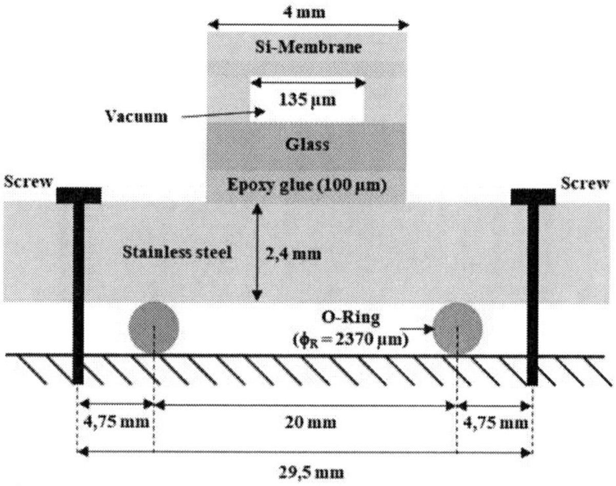

Figure 9. Cross section view of the device used for the simulation model.

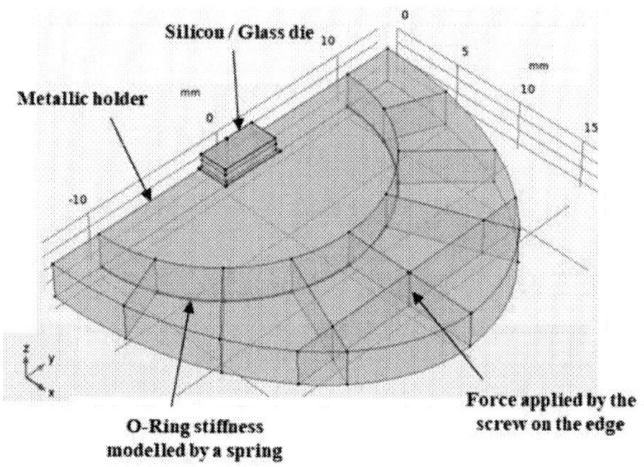

Figure 10. COMSOL 3D view of the half-simulated device. The membrane length is along x axis.

The pressure response of the device is simulated for four different cases, corresponding to different mechanical stresses on the sensor's holder (Figure 11). The case *#1* corresponds to configuration *#F*, in which the sensor's holder is not subjected to a mechanical stress, as the screw tightening force is zero and the pressure is identical at both sides of the sensor's holder. The case *#2* is associated with the configuration *#S*, in which the sensor's holder is subjected to two types of stresses that deform it, that is, (a) the differential pressure applied on the central part of the sensor's holder (inside the O-ring) and, (b) the screw tightening force. The cases *#3* and *#4* allow isolating respectively the effect of the differential pressure and the screw tightening force on the deformation of the sensor's holder (in case *#3*, the pressure is not applied to the membrane surface).

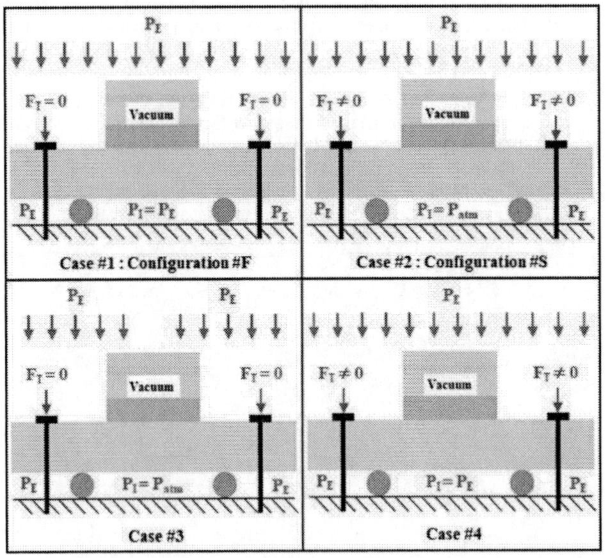

Figure 11. Description of the four studied simulation cases.

The simulations are performed with $P_E = 1$ bar absolute and $P_E = 2$ bar absolute. Table II shows the results obtained for the stress values at the centre of the membrane and at its surface. The stress extracted is the differential stress $\sigma_{xx} - \sigma_{yy}$, that is the stress along the length of the membrane minus the stress along its width. The pressure sensitivity S_p of the sensor is, as a first approximation, directly proportional to S_σ defined by the relationship (1).

$$S_\sigma = (\sigma_{xx} - \sigma_{yy})_{P_E = 2\,\text{bar}} - (\sigma_{xx} - \sigma_{yy})_{P_E = 1\,\text{bar}} \quad (1)$$

TABLE II. SIMULATED STRESS ON THE SURFACE OF THE MEMBRANE AND FOR X = Y = 0 (CENTER OF THE MEMBRANE)

$\sigma_{xx} - \sigma_{yy}$	$P_E = 1$ bar	$P_E = 2$ bar	S_σ
Case *#1* (Configuration *#F*)	2.86 MPa	5.72 MPa	2.86 MPa/bar
Case *#2* (Configuration *#S*)	14.73 MPa	18.47 MPa	3.74 MPa/bar
Case *#3*	0	0.86 MPa	0.86 MPa/bar
Case *#4*	14.73 MPa	17.59 MPa	2.86 MPa/bar

The case *#1* provides the reference sensitivity of 2.86 MPa/bar, which corresponds to the sensitivity obtained when only the membrane deforms with the applied pressure. In this case, the offset ($P_E = 1$ bar absolute) is not zero since there is vacuum in the cavity below the membrane. When we add to case *#1* the tightening of the screws that deform the sensor's holder (case *#4*), the offset increases significantly (≅ + 12 MPa) but the pressure sensitivity is unchanged. The increase in pressure sensitivity (case *#2*) of 0.88 MPa/bar (≅ +30%) comes from the deformation of the sensor's holder (case *#3*), which causes the deformation of the Silicon-Glass chip and in turn, of the membrane. These results are consistent with the measurement results, even if the simulated increase magnitude is much lower than the measured magnitude (30% instead of more than 100 %). More Multiphysics simulations would be necessary to identify the origin of this discrepancy.

Preliminary characterization is performed by increasing the thickness of the glass substrate (from 0.5 mm to 2 mm) in order to enhance the mechanical stiffness of the Silicon-Glass chip. Pressure measurements show an increase in pressure sensitivity of only 20% when moving from the configuration *#F* to the configuration *#S*.

VI. CONCLUSION

The development of new packaged sensors for the monitoring of blast waves is challenging. We have previously developed a transducer using silicon micro-membrane and piezoresistive gauges to reduce the reaction time compared to one achieved by commercial sensors and we have experimentally validated the dynamic behaviour of sensor using a shock tube. However, we identified undesirable effects, that lead to large drift after few microseconds.

In order to understand the impact of the packaging in the pressure sensor performances, we studied the sensor responses under static pressure and for various packaging configurations. Measurement results have shown that the sensor sensitivity to pressure is increased by more than 100% when the sensor's holder is deformed by applied pressure. Simulation results obtained from COMSOL software confirmed this effect (even if the simulated magnitude is not of 100%, but of 30% only) and indicated that it is related to the holder mechanical deformation transferred to the silicon-glass die and to the membrane. The effect is large as the membrane deflection under pressure is very low (few nm/ bar). Preliminary characterizations with thicker glass substrate have shown a reduction by a factor six of the effect of holder deformation on the sensor pressure sensitivity.

In future works, the COMSOL model will be used to reduce the impact of the packaging on the dynamic responses of the pressure sensors to blast waves.

Acknowledgment

This work was partially funded by CEA-DAM, through the LICUR (joint Laboratory between CEA-DAM and CNRS-LAAS) and by Occitanie Region (France) and was supported by LAAS-CNRS micro and nanotechnologies platform members of the French RENATECH network.

References

[1] L. Walter, "Air-blast and the Science of Dynamic Pressure Measurements," Sound and Vibration, vol. 38, no. 12, pp. 10-17, December 2004.

[2] M. Chalnot, P. Pons, and H. Aubert, "Frequency Bandwidth of Pressure Sensors Dedicated to Blast Experiments," Sensors, vol. 22, no. 10, p. 3790, May 2022, https://doi.org/10.3390/s22103790.

[3] N. Wu et al., "Low-cost rapid miniature optical pressure sensors for blast wave measurements," Optic Express, vol. 19, no. 11, p. 10797, May 2011, doi: 10.1364/OE.19.010797.

[4] X. Zou et al., "Ultrafast Fabry–Perot fiber-optic pressure sensors for multimedia blast event measurements," Applied Optics, vol. 52, no. 6, p. 124820, February 2013, doi: 10.1364/AO.52.001248.

[5] C. Chu, J. Wang, and J. Qiu, "Miniature High-Frequency Response, High-Pressure-Range Dynamic Pressure Sensor Based on All-Silica Optical Fiber Fabry-Perot Cavity," IEEE Sensors Journal, vol. 21, no. 12, pp. 13296–13304, June 2021, doi: 10.1109/JSEN.2021.3068456.

[6] J. Riondet et al., "Shock Tube Characterization of Air Blast Pressure Sensor Based on Ultra-Miniature Silicon Membrane and Piezoresistive Gauges," Micro and Nano Engineering Conference, Turin, Italy, Sep. 2021.

[7] K. Sanchez et al., "Design, Fabrication and Characterization of a Novel Piezoresistive Pressure Sensor for Blast Waves Monitoring," International Conference on Sensor Device Technologies and Applications, Athens, Greece, Nov. 2021, pp. 47–52, ISSN: 2308-3514, ISBN: 978-1-61208-918-8.

Positioning Using Visible Light Communication Footprints

Paula Louro, Manuela Vieira, Manuel Augusto Vieira
DEETC/ISEL/IPL,
R. Conselheiro Emídio Navarro, 1959-007
Lisboa, Portugal
CTS-UNINOVA
Quinta da Torre, Monte da Caparica, 2829-516,
Caparica, Portugal

e-mail: plouro@deetc.isel.pt, mv@isel.ipl.pt, mv@isel.pt

Pedro Vieira
DEETC/ISEL/IPL,
R. Conselheiro Emídio Navarro, 1959-007
Lisboa, Portugal
Instituto das Telecomunicações
Instituto Superior Técnico, 1049-001,
Lisboa, Portugal
pvieira@isel.pt

Abstract— **Global Positioning System (GPS) cannot manage indoor positioning because the strong attenuation of the signal by walls and infrastructures results in a lack of signal or poor accuracy. Oher technologies based on RF, optical, magnetic or acoustic signals can be used for this purpose. Visible Light Communication (VLC) is a good alternative, providing good positioning accuracy. In this work, we propose a system using commercial tri-chromatic LEDs that illuminate and transmit modulated data that is used to infer the user's position. The receiver is based on a dedicated pinpin heterostructure photodiode with selective response in the visible spectrum. The positioning system includes multiple, identical navigation cells. In each cell, the optical pattern created by the VLC transmitters defines specific spatial areas which are assigned to different optical excitations determining the cell footprints. The photocurrent signal measured by the photodetector is demodulated and decoded to provide identification of input optical excitations and enable position detection. The footprint model is evaluated under Line of Sight (LoS) conditions, assuming the Lambertian model for the LED light distribution. The channel gain is computed adjusting the model parameters related to gains and losses to experimental data to calibrate the system. Bit decoding algorithm provides data transmission recovery. Experimental data obtained in a prototype model scale confirms that the proposed VLC architecture is appropriate for indoor positioning application.**

Keywords- Visible Light Communication; positioning;white LEDs; navigation cell; footprint map.

I. INTRODUCTION

Indoor positioning can be addressed by several technologies based on the use of different techniques [1][2]. Visible Light Communication (VLC) is a good alternative since white lighting solutions based on LEDs have become commonplace in most buildings.

VLC is a technology based on the use of visible light in the 400 to 800 THz for the visible light from 750 to 400 nm [3][4]. The main advantages of VLC are its wide bandwidth, free and unlicensed spectrum, lack of electromagnetic interference, communication security, human health safety, and compatibility with other technologies. VLC systems use modulated LEDs to transmit information and single photodiodes or camera devices in the receiver units.

In this paper, we propose the use of a multilayered a:SiC:H [5] device to perform the photodetection of the optical signals generated by white trichromatic RGB LEDs [6], [7]. The system was designed for guidance [8][9], and the emitters of each white LED were specifically modulated at precise frequencies and coding bit sequences [10][11]. The proposed lighting and positioning/guidance system involves wireless communication, computer-based algorithms, smart sensor and optical sources network, which constitutes a transdisciplinary approach framed in cyber-physical systems. The paper is organized as follows. After the introduction (Section I), the VLC system architecture is presented in Section II. In Section III, models for the footprint characterization using both geometrical and propagation assumptions are analyzed. In Section IV, the communication protocol and the encoding/decoding techniques are analyzed and discussed. At last, conclusions are addressed in Section V.

II. VLC SYSTEM SPECIFICATIONS

The specifications od the VLC system described in this paper include the characterization of the transmitter and receiver units, respectively with the optical signal sources and the dedicated photodiode. Besides, the characterization of the channel will also be discussed using the Lambertian model do describe light propagation from the LEDs in Line-of Sight conditions.

A. *VLC Transmitter and Receiver Units*

The transmitter uses commercial white LEDs with tri-chromatic emitters (red, green, and blue). In the lamp, four white LEDs are arranged in a square geometry with a quadrangular topology (Figure 1).

Only one emitter of each white LED is modulated. Other emitters operate only with DC current to provide white color illumination [12]. In this specific case, the modulated emitters are the red emitters of the LEDs on the left side of the lamp, and the blue emitters on the right side.

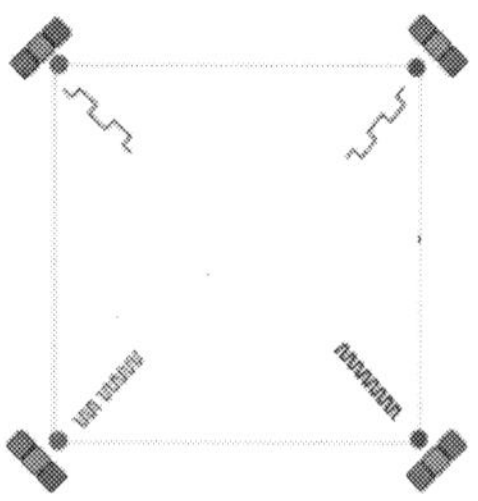

Figure 1. Configuration of the VLC emitter with 4 RGB white LEDs.

The pinpin photodiode of the receiver unit transduces light into an electrical signal that can be demodulated and decoded. This device is a monolithic heterojunction composed of two pin structures based on a-Si:H and a-SiC:H built on a glass substrate and sandwiched between two transparent electrical contacts. The front structure based on a-SiC:H absorbs mainly the short wavelengths (violet and blue), while the back structure based on a-Si:H absorbs the long waveleng8ths (red). Intermediate wavelengths as green light are absorbed by both pin structures, A reverse bias (-8 V) and short wavelength (400 nm) illumination are used to tune the device selectivity externally.

B. *Channel*

LEDs are modeled as Lambertian sources with uniform distribution of luminance in all directions, and luminous intensity dependent on the direction. The luminous intensity for a Lambertian source is given by the following equation [13]:

$$I(\phi) = I_N \cos^m(\phi) \qquad (1)$$

where m is the order derived from a Lambertian pattern, I_N is the maximum luminous intensity in the axial direction and ϕ is the angle of irradiance. The Lambertian order m is given by:

$$m = -\frac{\ln(2)}{\ln(\cos(\phi_{1/2}))} \qquad (2)$$

As the half intensity angle ($\phi_{1/2}$) is of 60º, the Lambertian order m is 1. The light signal is received by the photodetector, generates a binary sequence of the received signals and convert data into the original format. It is assumed Line of Sight (LoS) conditions, which considers that the signal propagation occurs in a direct path from the source to the receiver.

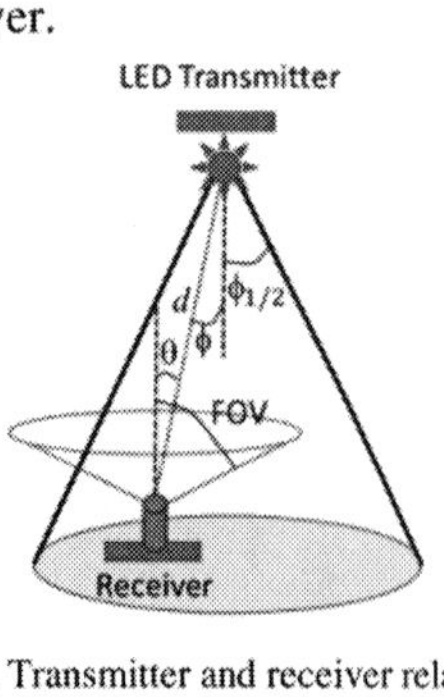

Figure 2. Transmitter and receiver relative position.

Figure 2 shows the relative position of the transmitter and receiver units with specification of the geometrical parameters needed to infer the signal coverage of the LED in the illuminated indoors space [14].

The channel gain (G) of this VLC link given by equation [15]:

$$G = \frac{(m+1)A}{2\pi d^2} I_N \cos^m(\emptyset)\cos(\theta) \qquad (3)$$

where A is the area of the photodetector, d the distance between the emitter and the receiver, and FOV the field of view of the detector (angular extension for signal detection).

Figure 3 illustrates the coverage map produced when only the red and blue emitters of each LED are used for data transmission.

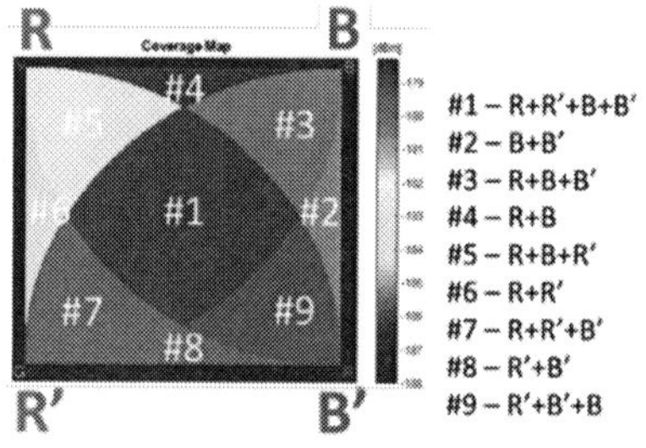

Figure 3. Coverage map of the fine-grain footprint inside the navigation cell, considering as VLC optical sources the top red and bottom blue emitters.

The optical signal produced by each modulated LED confers a maximum of delivered power signal at the central region of the cell, that receives contribution from four modulated channels. The regions at the corners contain optical signals from three LEDs, exhibiting a decrease on the received power signal, while the side regions correspond to the lowest values of received power. Each of these regions constitute footprints of the delivered power. Each footprint region labelled as #1, #2, …, #9 is assigned to the correspondent optical excitation illustrated on the right side of Figure 3.

III. POSITIONING ALGORITHM

The positioning algorithm is based on the identification of the navigation cell and on the footprint where the mobile user is located. Thus, bit coding of the information transmitted by each modulated emitter and bit decoding at the receiver is mandatory to infer from the multiplexed signal at the receiver the input optical signals and the correspondent identification of the cell and footprint.

A. *Coding and modulation*

The data is converted into byte format and then converted into light signals emitted by the VLC transmitter. On–Off Keying (OOK) modulation is used to modulate the data bit stream. To ensure proper coding and decoding at the transmitter and receiver units, the data format used to transmit information, namely the length of each frame, the blocks that make up each word and its contents, is previously defined. The communication codes use 64 word frames. The structure of the data frame used in each channel is displayed in Figure 4. Transmitted data can have a passive role (standard mode) with continuous transmission of lamp identification to ensure positioning, or an active role (request mode) transmitting additional information to guide the user.

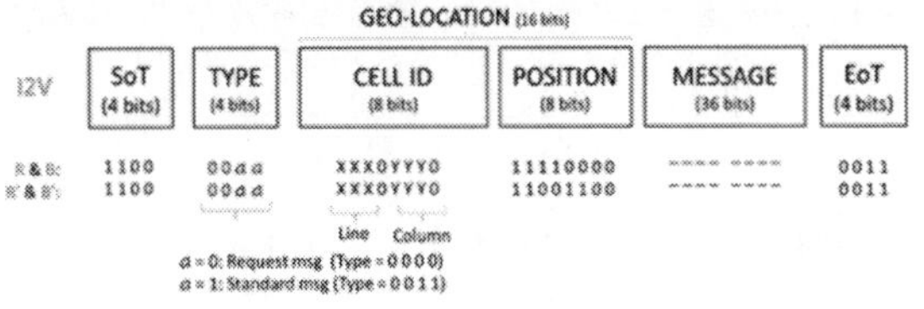

Figure 4. Data frame structure the coded word.

The TYPE block (4 bits) is used to identify the type of transmitted message, either if it is to acknowledge the reception of any request or to transmit updated information. This block is transmitted equally by all active emitters of the transmitter (R, R', B and B'). The GEO-LOCATION block of the I2V channel has 16 bits and can be divided into two sub-blocks. A block of 8 bits with the identification of the cell (CELL ID block) and a second block of 8 bits with the position inside the cell (POSITION block). The block labelled as CELL ID is a word of 8 bits. It provides the identification of the unit navigation cell. The format of the word code is XXX0YYY0, where XXX addresses the line and YYY the column of the cell. The block POSITION (8 bits) is encoded with 4 bits set to 1 and 4 bits set to 0 in channels R and B, while, for the bottom emitters, R' and B', the frequency of this word is doubled, corresponding to the sequence of 2 bits set to 1, 2 bits set to 0, 2 bits set to 1 and 2 bits set to 0. This block provides accurate position information inside the navigation cell. The MESSAGE block (36 bits) contains different blocks depending on the type of message being transmitted. In the request mode it contains info to guide the user inside the building and additional bits reserved for future transmission specifications. In acknowledge mode the block is initially set to null, containing also additional reserved bits.

B. Bit decoding

In the receiver unit, it is necessary to decode the photocurrent signal, which identifies the footprint inside the cell and, therefore, enables the determination of the position. To establish this assignment, a calibration curve is defined beforehand. In Figure 5, the calibration curve is plotted with 16 different photocurrent thresholds resulting from the combination of the four modulated signals from the white VLC emitter.

Different levels of photocurrent were generated by adjusting the driving current of the LED emitters. On the top it is displayed the waveform of the emitters modulation state used to produce the calibration curve. The right hand side of Figure 5 illustrates how each footprint corresponds to a photocurrent level. The correct use of this calibration curve demands a periodic retransmission of curve to ensure a accurate correspondence to the output signal and an accurate decoding of the transmitted information.

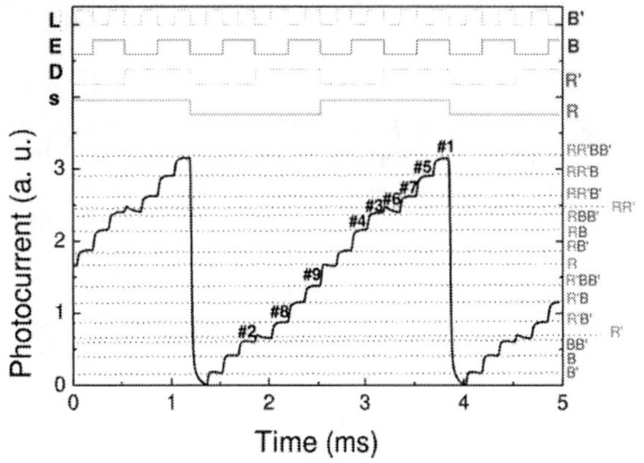

Figure 5. Calibration front photocurrent signal using two red and two blue optical signals modulated with multiple frequencies.

IV. RESULTS AND DISCUSSION

In Figure 6, the photocurrent signal measured by the mobile receiver unit is depicted at two different locations within the cell covered by RR'BB' and R'BB' optical signals, which correspond, respectively, to footprints labelled #1 and #9.

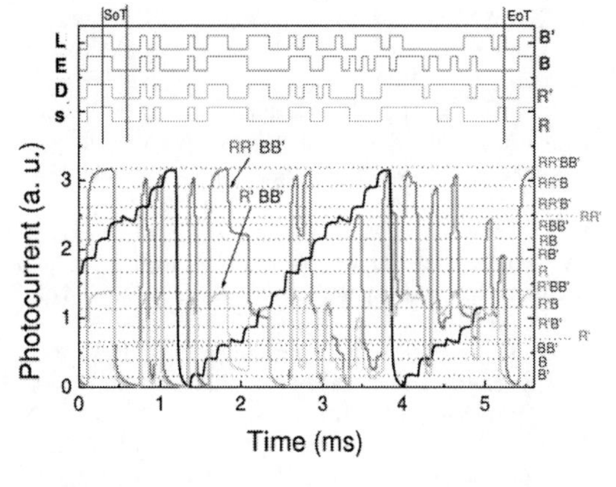

Figure 6. Photocurrent signal measured by the mobile receiver unit at footprints #1 and #9 inside the navigation cell (RR'BB' and R'BB'). The calibration curve is displayed in the background.

On the right side of the graph it is stated the optical state assigned to each step of the calibration curve. Frame synchronization is detected by the blocks SOT and EoT. Due to the simultaneous operation of all emitters in both measurements, either inside footprints #1 and #9 (RR'BB' and R'BB'), the presence of these blocks corresponds to maximum values of the photocurrent. To decode the photocurrent levels, the calibration curve is used to identify which emitters are active during the duration period of each bit. Input optical signals are decoded based on the observed correspondence between the different thresholds of the measured signal and the calibration steps. When threshold levels are close, decoding errors are more likely, which requires error control techniques.

V. CONCLUSIONS

In this paper, a VLC system for indoor positioning and guidance was presented. A theoretical analysis of irradiation patterns is presented to establish the footprints of the cells and support the position accuracy of the proposed system.

The Lambertian model was used to describe the light distribution. Each footprint of the cell was predicted using the channel gain model of the transmitter-receiver link.

Predicted results of the MatLab simulations were supported by experimental data measured with a laboratory prototype. Future work will comprise a more detailed and complete description of the decoding methodology.

ACKNOWLEDGMENT

This work was sponsored by FCT – Fundação para a Ciência e a Tecnologia, within the Research Unit CTS – Center of Technology and systems, reference UIDB/00066/2020 and IPL/2022/POSEIDON_ISEL.

REFERENCES

[1] R. Mautz, "Overview of Current Indoor Positioning Systems", Geodesy Cartogr., vol. 35, pp. 18–22, 2009.

[2] Y. Gu, A. Lo, and I. Niemegeers, "A Survey of Indoor Positioning Systems for Wireless Personal Networks," IEEE Commun. Surv. Tutor., vol. 11, pp. 13–32, 2009.

[3] A. M. Căilean and M. Dimian, "Current Challenges for Visible Light Communications Usage in Vehicle Applications: A Survey", IEEE Communications Surveys & Tutorials, vol. 19, no. 4, pp. 2681-2703, 2017.

[4] M. Z. Chowdhury, M. T. Hossan, A. Islam, and Y. M Jang, "A Comparative Survey of Optical Wireless Technologies: Architectures and Applications", IEEE Access, vol. 6, pp. 9819-9840, 2018.

[5] P. Louro, et al, "Optical demultiplexer based on an a-SiC:H voltage controlled device", Phys. Status Solidi C, vol. 7, no. 3–4, pp. 1188–1191, 2010.

[6] M. Vieira, M. A. Vieira, P. Louro, V. Silva, and P. Vieira, "Optical signal processing for indoor positioning using a-SiC:H technology", Opt. Eng., vol 55, no. 10, pp. 107105-1-107105-6, 2016.

[7] M. A. Vieira, M. Vieira, P. Louro, and P. Vieira, "Cooperative vehicular communication systems based on visible light communication," Opt. Eng., vol. 57, no. 7, pp. 076101-, 2018.

[8] P. Louro, V. Silva, M. A. Vieira, and M. Vieira, "Viability of the use of an a-SiC:H multilayer device in a domestic VLC application", Phys. Status Solidi C, vol, 11, no. 11–12, pp. 1703–1706, 2014.

[9] P. Louro, M. Vieira,1 and M. A. Vieira, "Geolocalization and navigation by visible light communication to address automated logistics control," Opt. Eng. **61**(1), 016104 (2022), doi: 10.1117/1.OE.61.1.016104.

[10] P. Louro, J. Costa, M. A. Vieira, and M. Vieira, "Optical Communication Applications based on white LEDs", J. Luminescence, vol. 191, pp. 122-125, 2017.

[11] M. Vieira, M. A. Vieira, I. Rodrigues, V. Silva, and P. Louro, "Photonic Amorphous Pi'n/pin SiC Optical Filter Under Controlled Near UV Irradiation", Sensors & Transducers, vol. 184, no. 1, pp. 123-129, 2015.

[12] P. Louro, M. Vieira, and M. A. Vieira, "Indoors Geolocation Based on Visible Light Communication", Sensors & Transducers, vol. 245, no. 6, pp. 57-64, 2020.

[13] Y. Zhu, W. Liang, J. Zhang, and Y. Zhang, "Space-Collaborative Constellation Designs for MIMO Indoor Visible Light Communications," IEEE Photonics Technology Letters, vol. 27, no. 15, pp. 1667–1670, 2015.

[14] S. I. Raza, et al, "Optical Wireless Channel Characterization For Indoor Visible Light Communications", Indian Journal of Science and Technology, vol 8, no. 22, pp. 1 – 9, 2015.

[15] Y. Qiu, H.-H. Chen, and W.-X. Meng, "Channel modeling for visible light communications - a survey", Wirel. Commun. and Mob. Comput., vol. 16, pp. 2016–2034, 2016.

Simultaneous Localization, Mapping and Moving-Object Tracking Using Helmet-Mounted LiDAR for Micro-Mobility

Ibuki Yoshida, Akihiko Yoshida
Graduate School of Science and Engineering
Doshisha University
Kyotanabe, Kyoto, Japan
e-mail: ctwg0157@mail4.doshisha.ac.jp

Masafumi Hashimoto, Kazuhiko Takahashi
Faculty of Science and Engineering
Doshisha University
Kyotanabe, Kyoto, Japan
e-mail: {mhashimo, katakaha}@mail.doshisha.ac.jp

***Abstract*— This paper presents a method of Simultaneous Localization, Mapping and Tracking of Moving Objects (SLAMTMO) using a Light Detection And Ranging sensor (LiDAR) mounted on a smart helmet worn by a vehicle rider. This technology can be used to active safety for micro-mobility, such as bicycles, e-bikes, and electric scooters, which are prioritized as personal commuters in the endemic society of coronavirus disease 2019. Distortion in the scan data from the LiDAR is corrected by estimating the helmet's pose (three-dimensional position and attitude angle) based on the information from Normal Distributions Transform (NDT)-based SLAM and an inertial measurement unit. The static and moving-object scan data, which originate from static and moving objects in the environments, respectively, are classified by subtracting the environment map generated by NDT-based SLAM from the LiDAR current scan data. The moving scan data are used for TMO based on a Bayesian filter, whereas the static scan data are used for point-cloud mapping. The experimental results in a road environment of our university campus show the effectiveness of the proposed SLAMTMO method.**

Keywords*—*helmet LiDAR; SLAM; moving-object tracking; micro-mobility.

I. INTRODUCTION

There have been numerous studies on active safety and autonomous driving in the field of Intelligent Transportation Systems (ITS) [1]. In the field of last-mile automation, there has also been a flourishing study on delivery robots [2]. The environmental map building using Simultaneous Localization And Mapping (SLAM) technology [3, 4] and Tracking of Moving Objects (TMO), such as cars, cyclists and pedestrians [5, 6], are important issues for autonomous driving and active safety of vehicles and mobile robots. Many related studies have been using cameras, radars, and Light Detection And Ranging (LiDAR). In this paper, we focus on SLAMTMO with a vehicle-mounted LiDAR.

To build a three-dimensional (3D) point-cloud map in community road environments, we presented a mapping method using car-mounted LiDAR based on Normal Distributions Transform (NDT)-Graph SLAM [7]. Using motorcycle-mounted LiDAR, we also proposed a method of 3D point-cloud mapping [8]. Moreover, we presented a TMO method utilizing car and motorcycle-mounted LiDAR [9, 10].

Coronavirus disease 2019 has caused people to be highly resistant to utilizing conventional means of urban transportation, such as crowded trains and buses. Hence, to escape the three Cs' (closed spaces, crowded spaces, and close-contact settings), the use of single-seater "micro-mobility", such as bicycles, e-bikes, electric scooters, and personal mobilities, are on the increase for short-distance travel in urban cities. The demand for micro-mobility additionally increased in the endemic society.

Even though the frequency of traffic accidents involving micro-mobility increases, the R&D related to active safety for micro-mobility is far behind. As a result, we are studying surrounding environmental sensing for micro-mobility, such as environmental map building and moving-object recognition for active safety in sidewalks and streets.

In the case of micro-mobility systems, it is difficult to mount a large number of sensors on the vehicle body, as is the case with cars, because of size and theft concerns. Thus, it is desirable to mount small and easily detachable sensors on the handlebar of the micro-mobility or on the helmet worn by the micro-mobility rider. Our previous work [11] proposed a method of building a 3D point-cloud map in sidewalk and roadway environments using LiDAR attached to the rider's helmet (Helmet-Mounted LiDAR, HML) of a micro-mobility.

This paper presents a SLAMTMO method using HML. The SLAMTMO can not only build a 3D point-cloud map in dynamic and Global Navigation Satellite System (GNSS)-denied environments but also recognize moving objects, such as cars, two-wheelers, and pedestrians. This study is an extension of our previous works [10, 11] on SLAM-based environmental mapping using HML and TMO by motorcycle-mounted LiDAR, and these methods are integrated into our HML system.

Several studies have been accomplished on surrounding environmental sensing using HML. Indoor SLAM, in which people wearing helmets equipped with two-dimensional (2D) LiDAR or one-dimensional (1D) LiDAR walk around in building and factory environments, was presented [12–14]. Niforatos et al. [15] presented a method of skier detection using 1D LiDAR attached to ski helmets to reduce the risk of accidents on ski slopes. To the best of our knowledge, no studies have been conducted on environmental sensing in sidewalks and roadways using 3D LiDAR attached to the rider's helmet of a micro-mobility. Although there have been several studies on helmets with sensors (smart helmets) in the ITS fields [16], their use is limited to alcohol detection in motorcycle riders and collision-accident detection, as well as confirming rider safety after accidents.

The rest of this paper is organized as follows. Section II describes the experimental system. Section III overviews the SLAMTMO. Section IV explains the distortion correction method for the LiDAR scan data, and Section V presents the classification method for scan data related to static and moving objects. Section VI presents experimental results to verify the proposed method, followed by the conclusions and future works in Section VII.

II. EXPERIMENTAL SYSTEM

Figure 1 shows the overview of the smart helmet. The upper part of the helmet is equipped with a mechanical 64-layer LiDAR (Ouster, OS0-64) and an inertial measurement unit (IMU) (Xsens, MTi-300).

The HML has a maximum range of 55 m, a horizontal field of view of 360 ° with a resolution of 0.35 °, and a vertical field of view of 90 ° with a resolution of 1.4 °. LiDAR can obtain 1024 measurements (distance, direction, and reflected light intensity) every 1.56 ms (every 5.6 ° in the horizontal direction). Therefore, approximately 66,000 points of scan data are acquired in one rotation (360 ° observation) period (100 ms).

Attitude angle (roll and pitch angles) and angular velocity (roll, pitch, and yaw angular velocities) of the helmet are obtained from the IMU every 10 ms. The measurement error for the attitude angle is less than ± 0.3 °, and that of the angular velocity is less than ± 0.2 °/s.

The weight of the mechanical LiDAR is 0.5 kg, and the smart helmet is heavier and larger than usual helmets. Therefore, the LiDAR reduces the usability and practicability of the smart helmet. Moreover, it affects the performance of the helmet in the event of a crash. However, modern LiDAR technology [17] has been developing smaller, more lightweight, and lower power consumption solid-state LiDARs than mechanical LiDARs. The use of solid-state LiDARs will much improve the usability and practicability of the smart helmet.

III. OVERVIEW OF SLAMTMO

Figure 2 shows the sequence of SLAMTMO. For the environmental mapping and TMO, LiDAR scan data captured in the helmet coordinate system attached to the HML are mapped onto the world coordinate system using the self-pose (3D position and attitude angle) information of the helmet. For this, an accurate self-pose of the helmet is required. NDT-based SLAM [18] is utilized to estimate the self-pose in GNSS-denied environments.

For the i-th measurement point (i = 1, 2, ...n) in the LiDAR scan data, the position in the helmet coordinate system is denoted by $\boldsymbol{p}_{Hi}=(x_{Hi},y_{Hi},z_{Hi})^T$, and that in the world coordinate system by $\boldsymbol{p}_i=(x_i,y_i,z_i)^T$. The following relationship is then represented by the homogeneous transformation:

$$\begin{pmatrix}\boldsymbol{p}_i\\1\end{pmatrix}=\boldsymbol{T}(\boldsymbol{X})\begin{pmatrix}\boldsymbol{p}_{Hi}\\1\end{pmatrix} \quad (1)$$

where $\boldsymbol{X}=(x,y,z,\phi,\theta,\psi)^T$. $(x,y,z)^T$ and $(\phi,\theta,\psi)^T$ are the 3D position and attitude angle (roll, pitch, and yaw angles), respectively, of the helmet in the world coordinate system. $\boldsymbol{T}(\boldsymbol{X})$ is the following homogeneous transformation matrix:

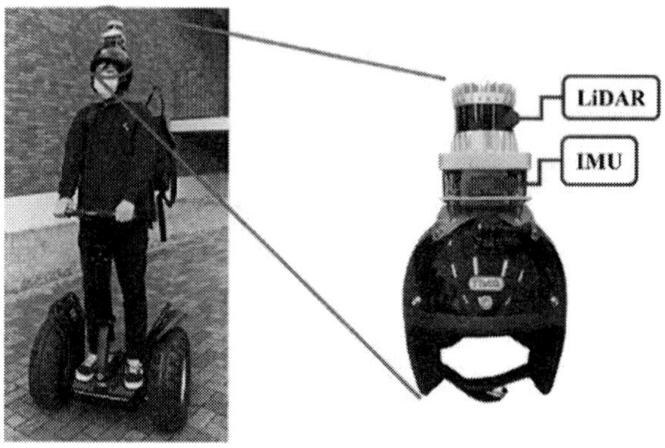

Figure 1. Overview of the experimental smart helmet.

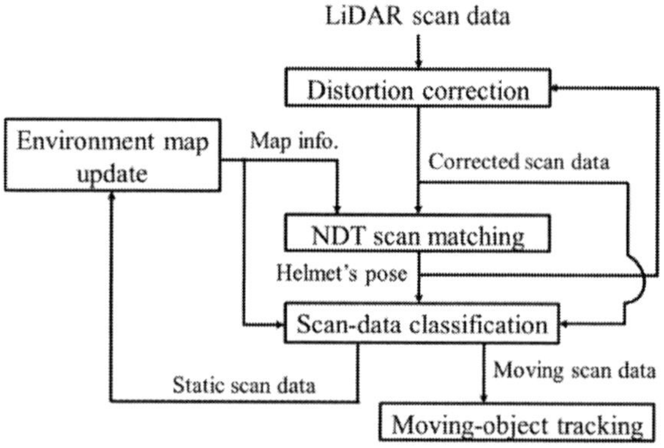

Figure 2. SLAMTMO sequence.

$$\boldsymbol{T}(\boldsymbol{X})=\begin{pmatrix}\cos\theta\cos\psi & \sin\phi\sin\theta\cos\psi-\cos\phi\sin\psi & \cos\phi\sin\theta\cos\psi+\sin\phi\sin\psi & x\\ \cos\theta\sin\psi & \sin\phi\sin\theta\sin\psi+\cos\phi\cos\psi & \cos\phi\sin\theta\sin\psi-\sin\phi\cos\psi & y\\ -\sin\theta & \sin\phi\cos\theta & \cos\phi\cos\theta & z\\ 0 & 0 & 0 & 1\end{pmatrix}$$

A voxel map with a cell size of 0.6 m per side is defined in the world coordinate system. In NDT-based SLAM, a normal distributions transformation is performed on the scan data obtained up to the previous time (referred to as environmental map) in each cell of the voxel map, and the mean and covariance of the scan data in each cell are calculated.

The current self-pose (position and attitude angle) $\boldsymbol{X}$ of the helmet is calculated by matching the scan data obtained at the current time (referred to as current scan data) with the environmental map. The current scan data are mapped onto the world coordinate system by performing a coordinate transformation according to (1) using the pose $\boldsymbol{X}$. They are then merged into the environmental map. By repeating this process every LiDAR scan period, the environmental map is built.

The shape of the moving object in TMO is represented by a cuboid with a width W, a length L, and a height H, as shown in Figure 3. The width W_{meas} and length L_{meas} of the moving object are extracted from the scan data related to a moving object (moving scan data). With these values, W and L of the moving object are estimated [10] by

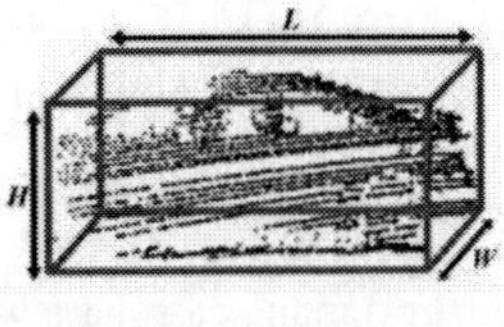

Figure 3. Cuboid around the tracked object (car).

$$\begin{cases} W(t) = W(t-1) + G(W_{meas} - W(t-1)) \\ L(t) = L(t-1) + G(L_{meas} - L(t-1)) \end{cases} \quad (2)$$

where G is the gain.

The height estimate H of the moving object is obtained from the height measurements of the moving scan data.

The Kalman filter is used to estimate the position and velocity of the moving object in the world coordinate system based on the centroid position of the rectangle estimated from (2). When applying the Kalman filter, it is assumed that the object is moving at an approximately constant velocity. In crowded environments, the rule-based data association method [19] is used to accurately match multiple moving objects with multiple moving scan data.

Because LiDAR scans laser in omnidirection, all the scan data within one scan cannot be obtained at a single location when the micro-mobility is moving or swinging, or when the rider's body is swinging. Therefore, if all of the scan data within one scan is transformed using the pose information of the helmet at the same time, distortion arises in the LiDAR scan data mapped in the world coordinate system. Since distortion causes inaccurate results in SLAM and TMO, distortion correction of the LiDAR scan data is required. The distortion-correction method is described in Section IV.

Scan data relating to static and moving objects (static and moving scan data) are used for SLAM and TMO, respectively. For this, accurate classification of static and moving scan data from entire scan data is required. The classification method is described in Section V.

IV. Distortion Correction of LiDAR Scan Data

The helmet's pose is determined every 100 ms (LiDAR scan period) using NDT-based SLAM. The scan data are acquired every 1.56 ms during one rotation of LiDAR. During LiDAR scanning, all the scan data within one scan cannot be obtained at a single location when the micro-mobility is moving or swinging, or when the rider's body is swinging. If all the scan data within one scan is transformed using the pose information of the helmet at the same time, distortion appears in the mapping of the LiDAR scan data onto the world coordinate system. Therefore, the distortion in the scan data is corrected by estimating the helmet's pose using the extended Kalman filter (EKF) every 1.56 ms, i.e., every LiDAR scan data are obtained.

In the EKF for correcting the scan-data distortion, a constant velocity model is used as the helmet motion. As shown in Figure 4, the translational velocity of the helmet in the helmet coordinate system (O_H-$x_H y_H z_H$) is denoted by (V_x, V_y, V_z), and the angular velocity (roll, pitch, and yaw angular velocities) by ($\dot{\phi}_H, \dot{\theta}_H, \dot{\psi}_H$). The following motion model of the helmet can be obtained assuming that the helmet moves at nearly constant translational and angular velocities:

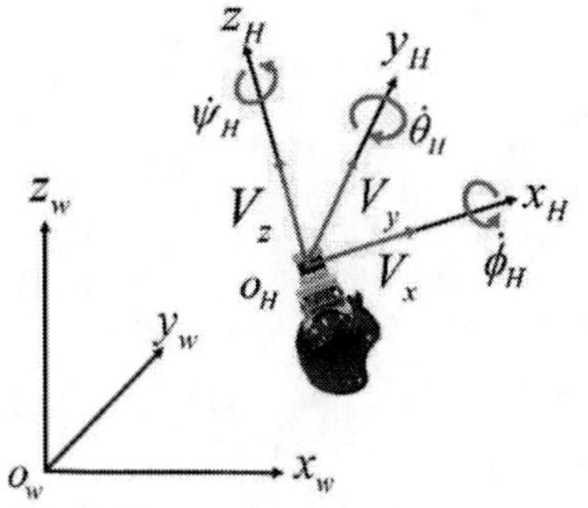

Figure 4. Notation related to the helmet motion.

$$\begin{pmatrix} x_{(t+1)} \\ y_{(t+1)} \\ z_{(t+1)} \\ \phi_{(t+1)} \\ \theta_{(t+1)} \\ \psi_{(t+1)} \\ V_{x(t+1)} \\ V_{y(t+1)} \\ V_{z(t+1)} \\ \dot{\phi}_{H(t+1)} \\ \dot{\theta}_{H(t+1)} \\ \dot{\psi}_{H(t+1)} \end{pmatrix} = \begin{pmatrix} x_{(t)} + a_{1(t)}\cos\theta_{(t)}\cos\psi_{(t)} \\ \quad + a_{2(t)}\{\sin\phi_{(t)}\sin\theta_{(t)}\cos\psi_{(t)} - \cos\phi_{(t)}\sin\psi_{(t)}\} \\ \quad + a_{3(t)}\{\cos\phi_{(t)}\sin\theta_{(t)}\cos\psi_{(t)} + \sin\phi_{(t)}\sin\psi_{(t)}\} \\ y_{(t)} + a_{1(t)}\cos\theta_{(t)}\sin\psi_{(t)} \\ \quad + a_{2(t)}\{\sin\phi_{(t)}\sin\theta_{(t)}\sin\psi_{(t)} + \cos\phi_{(t)}\cos\psi_{(t)}\} \\ \quad + a_{3(t)}\{\cos\phi_{(t)}\sin\theta_{(t)}\sin\psi_{(t)} - \sin\phi_{(t)}\cos\psi_{(t)}\} \\ z_{(t)} - a_{1(t)}\sin\theta_{(t)} + a_{2(t)}\sin\phi_{(t)}\cos\theta_{(t)} \\ \quad + a_{3(t)}\cos\phi_{(t)}\cos\theta_{(t)} \\ \phi_{(t)} + a_{4(t)} + \{a_{5(t)}\sin\phi_{(t)} + a_{6(t)}\cos\phi_{(t)}\}\tan\theta_{(t)} \\ \theta_{(t)} + \{a_{5(t)}\cos\phi_{(t)} - a_{6(t)}\sin\phi_{(t)}\} \\ \psi_{(t)} + \{a_{5(t)}\sin\phi_{(t)} + a_{6(t)}\cos\phi_{(t)}\}\dfrac{1}{\cos\theta_{(t)}} \\ V_{x(t)} + \tau w_{\dot{V}x} \\ V_{y(t)} + \tau w_{\dot{V}y} \\ V_{z(t)} + \tau w_{\dot{V}z} \\ \dot{\phi}_{H(t)} + \tau w_{\ddot{\phi}_H} \\ \dot{\theta}_{H(t)} + \tau w_{\ddot{\theta}_H} \\ \dot{\psi}_{H(t)} + \tau w_{\ddot{\psi}_H} \end{pmatrix} \quad (3)$$

where (x, y, z) and (ϕ, θ, ψ) are the position and attitude angle (roll, pitch, and yaw angles), respectively, of the helmet in the world coordinate system (O_w-$x_w y_w z_w$). ($w_{\dot{V}x}, w_{\dot{V}y}, w_{\dot{V}z}, w_{\ddot{\phi}_H}, w_{\ddot{\theta}_H}, w_{\ddot{\psi}_H}$) is the acceleration disturbance. τ is the LiDAR scan period. $a_1 = V_x\tau + \tau^2 w_{\dot{V}_x}/2$, $a_2 = V_y\tau + \tau^2 w_{\dot{V}y}/2$, $a_3 = V_z\tau + \tau^2 w_{\dot{V}_z}/2$, $a_4 = \dot{\phi}_H\tau + \tau^2 w_{\ddot{\phi}_H}/2$, $a_5 = \dot{\theta}_H\tau + \tau^2 w_{\ddot{\theta}_H}/2$, and $a_6 = \dot{\psi}_H\tau + \tau^2 w_{\ddot{\psi}_H}/2$.

Figure 5 shows the sequence of distortion correction. The LiDAR scan period (100 ms) is denoted as τ, the IMU observation period (10 ms) as $\Delta\tau_{IMU}$, and the scan data observation period (1.56 ms) as $\Delta\tau$. Here, the method for correcting the scan-data distortion obtained between time $(t-1)\tau$ and $t\tau$ is described [20].

Let us suppose that at the time $(t-1)\tau$, the pose of the helmet is calculated by NDT-based SLAM and estimated via EKF. The IMU data are obtained 10 times per LiDAR scan ($\tau = 10\Delta\tau_{IMU}$). Using the IMU data obtained every $\Delta\tau_{IMU}$, the EKF

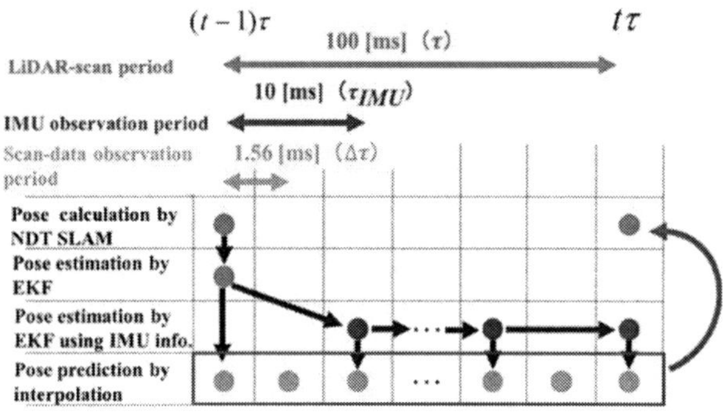

Figure 5. Sequence of distortion correction.

estimates the pose $\hat{X}(t-1,k)$ at the time $(t-1)\tau + k\Delta\tau_{IMU}$, where k = 0–10. Since the observation period $\Delta\tau_{IMU}$ of the IMU is 10 ms, and the scan-data observation period $\Delta\tau$ is 1.56 ms, the LiDAR scan data are obtained six times within the IMU observation period ($\Delta\tau_{IMU} = 6\Delta\tau$).

From the estimates, $\hat{X}(t-1,k)$ at the time $(t-1)\tau + k\Delta\tau_{IMU}$ and $\hat{X}(t-1,k+1)$ at $(t-1)\tau + (k+1)\Delta\tau_{IMU}$ the interpolation algorithm predicts the helmet's pose $\hat{X}(t-1,k,j)$ at $(t-1)\tau + k\Delta\tau_{IMU} + j\Delta\tau$ (where j = 1–5), at which the scan data are acquired.

The scan data $p_{Hi}(t-1,k,j)$ (where $i = 1, 2, \ldots, n$) obtained at $(t-1)\tau + k\Delta\tau_{IMU} + j\Delta\tau$ in the helmet coordinate system are transformed to $p_i(t-1,k,j)$ in the world coordinate system using Eq. (1) as follows:

$$\begin{pmatrix} p_i(t-1,k,j) \\ 1 \end{pmatrix} = T(\hat{X}(t-1,k,j)) \begin{pmatrix} p_{Hi}(t-1,k,j) \\ 1 \end{pmatrix} \quad (4)$$

Using the pose estimate $\hat{X}(t-1,10)$ at $t\tau$ $(= (t-1)\tau + 10\Delta\tau_{IMU})$, the scan data $p_i(t-1,k,j)$ obtained by Eq. (4) is again transformed into the scan data $p^*_{Hi}(t)$ in the helmet coordinate system at $t\tau$ by

$$\begin{pmatrix} p^*_{Hi}(t) \\ 1 \end{pmatrix} = T(\hat{X}(t-1,10))^{-1} \begin{pmatrix} p_i(t-1,k,j) \\ 1 \end{pmatrix} \quad (5)$$

$p^*_{Hi}(t)$ is the scan data that correct distortion at $t\tau$. Using the corrected scan data, SLAMTMO is performed.

V. CLASSIFICATION OF STATIC AND MOVING SCAN DATA

For SLAM, the moving scan data have to be eliminated and the static scan data have to be extracted from the whole LiDAR scan data. TMO conversely requires the removal of static scan data and the extraction of moving scan data from the whole LiDAR scan data. For this, accurate classification of static and moving scan data is required. Although the classification is usually performed based on the occupancy grid method, in practical environments, LiDAR noises and outliers frequently cause misclassification.

We utilize an environment map built by NDT-based SLAM to minimize the misclassification. We call this approach environment map subtraction (EMS)-based classification or dynamic background subtraction-based method [10]. Figure 6 shows the EMS-based classification method. In this method, we subtract the environment map built by NDT-based SLAM from the current scan data to remove as much static scan data as possible from the entire LiDAR scan data. The scan data extracted using the EMS-based method are mapped onto a grid map. The cell on the grid map is a square with a side-length of 0.3 m. A cell in which scan data exist is called an occupied cell. For the moving scan data, the time to occupy the same cell is short (less than 0.7 s in this paper), whereas for the static scan data, the time is long (not less than 0.7 s). Therefore, by using the occupancy grid method based on the cell occupancy time [19], cells occupied by moving scan data (or static scan data) can be detected as moving cells (or static cells).

Because an object takes multiple cells, adjacent occupied cells are clustered. Then, clustered moving cells (or static cells) are obtained as a moving cell group (or static cell group). The scan data contained in the moving cell group are finally decided as the moving scan data. The static scan data are extracted by subtracting the moving scan data from the LiDAR current scan data.

The LiDAR field of view also moves along with the micro-mobility movement. Even though an object that recently enters the LiDAR field of view is static, it is misclassified as a moving object because the cell occupancy time is short. To address this problem, new-observation cells are defined on the grid map, which correspond to the new field of view of the LiDAR. The time of cells entering the LiDAR field of view (T_{NC}) and the cell occupancy time (T_{OC}) are measured, and the occupancy time rate (α) is calculated by $\alpha = T_{OC} / T_{NC}$. Cells in which α is 10% or more are determined to be new-observation cells and then considered moving cells. This can minimize the false classification of static objects recently entering the LiDAR field of view as moving objects.

The scan data in the environment map are sparser in the areas in front of the micro-mobility and in the occlusion areas. Therefore, the static scan data likewise exist in a sparse state

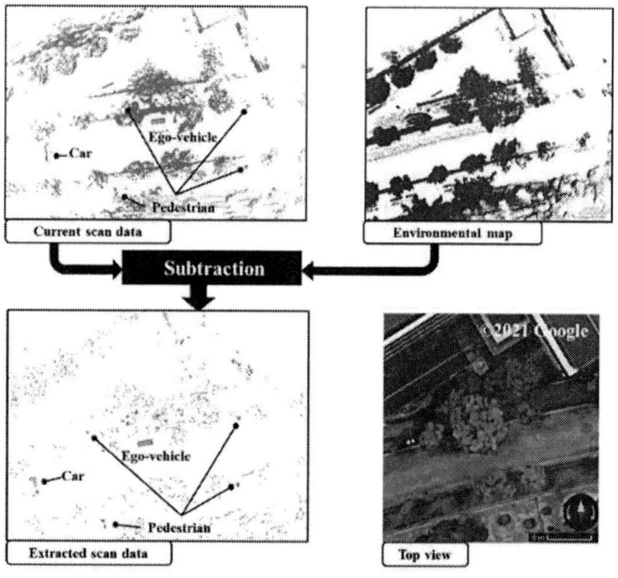

Figure 6. Sequence of EMS-based classification (top view).

when the environment map is subtracted from the current scan data. If the scan data, sparsely extracted based on the EMS-based method, are mapped onto a grid map, it may be erroneously determined as a moving cell.

To overcome this issue, the scan data removed by the EMS-based method are additionally mapped onto the grid map as static cells. As a result, sparse static scan data that tend to be moving cells and static scan data that are removed by the EMS-based method are both mapped onto the grid map. Neighboring cells, in which these static scan data are occupied, are clustered, and the cell group is then determined to be a static cell group. Accordingly, sparse static scan data are correctly determined as static scan data by the occupancy grid method.

VI. FUNDAMENTAL EXPERIMENTS

A micro-mobility was moved on our university-campus road, as shown in Figure 7, and SLAMTMO is performed. The traveling distance of the mobility is approximately 500 m, and the maximum speed is approximately 30 km/h. Figure 8 shows the attitude angle and angular velocity of the helmet during driving, which are observed by the IMU.

Figure 8 shows the TMO results. In Figure 9(b), the blue rectangle indicates the assessed size of the moving object, and the blue stick indicates the moving direction of the moving object obtained from the velocity estimate. The black (or red) dots reveal the scan data removed (or extracted) from the LiDAR scan data using the EMS-based method.

The micro-mobility is moved three times along the path shown in Figure 7 (a). Then, 111 moving objects (106 pedestrians and five cars) are tracked. The TMO performance is examined under the following two cases:

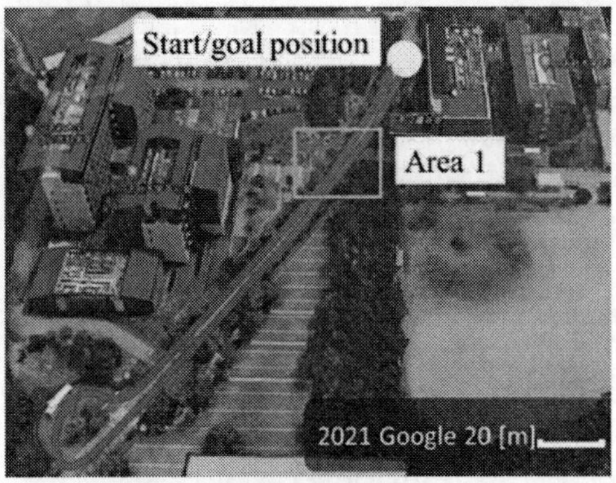

(a) Top view

(b) Side view

Figure 7. Photo of experimental environment.

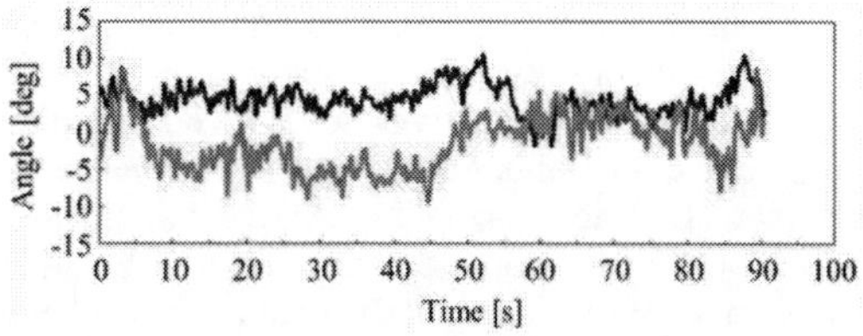

(a) Roll (black) and Pitch(red) angles

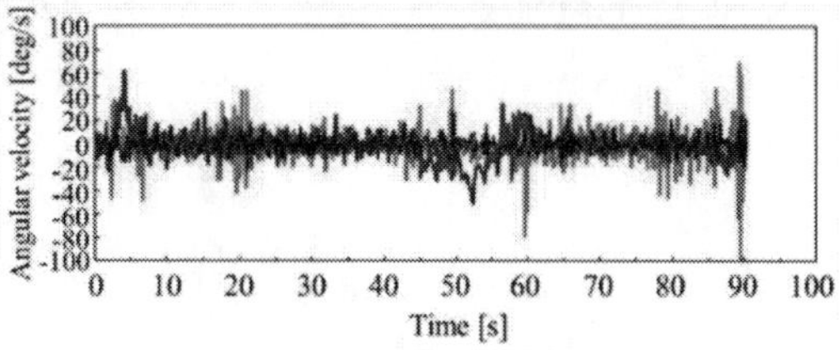

(b) Roll (black), pitch (red) and yaw (blue) angular velocities

Figure 8. Attitude angle and angular velocity of helmet.

(a) Photo of area 1

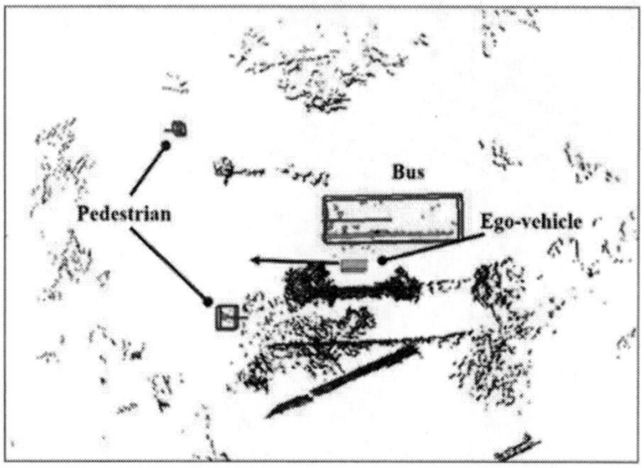

(b) Estimated track and size of the moving objects in area 1

Figure 9. Tracking result (top view).

- Case 1: Tracking with distortion correction of LiDAR scan data and EMS-based classification method (proposed method)
- Case 2: Tracking without using either method.

As the result, in case 1, 109 objects (104 pedestrians and five cars) can be successfully tracked, and two pedestrians cannot be tracked. In case 2, conversely, 103 objects (98 pedestrians and five cars) can be successfully tracked, and eight pedestrians cannot be tracked. Pedestrians who are not being tracked are mistakenly classified as static objects. From these results, our proposed method gives better TMO accuracy.

Figure 10 shows the SLAM result estimated by the proposed method (case 1). In the SLAM, the mapping accuracy can be evaluated by the pose accuracy. Therefore, the error of position estimate of the helmet at the goal position is measured by a GNSS/LiDAR positioning system set at the goal position. Table I reveals the result, in which the micro-mobility is moved three times on the road shown in Figure 7. From the table, the proposed method (case 1) provides the SLAM accuracy better than case 2.

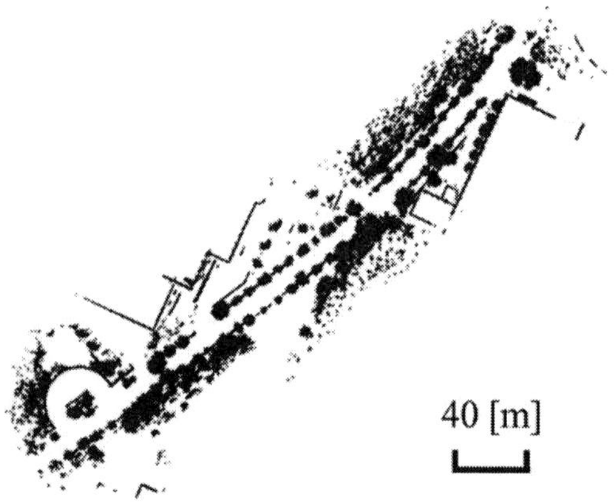

(a) Overall map (top view)

(b) Map in area 1 (bird's-eye view)

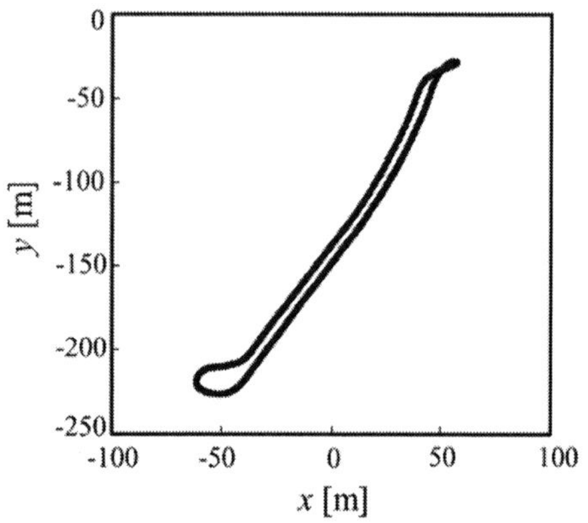

(c) Position estimate

Figure 10. SLAM result.

TABLE I. ERROR OF POSITION ESTIMATE OF HELMET AT GOAL POSITION.

	Case 1	Case 2
Exp 1	0.23 m	5.91 m
Exp 2	1.93 m	15.10 m
Exp 3	0.71 m	6.03 m

TABLE II. PROCESSING TIME OF SLAMTMO (CASE 1)

	Distortion correction and NDT SLAM	Scan data classification	Environment map update, moving-object tracking, and others	Total
Exp 1	2180 ms	801 ms	33 ms	3014 ms
Exp 2	2068 ms	719 ms	30 ms	2817 ms
Exp 3	1815 ms	659 ms	33 ms	2507 ms
Mean	2021 ms	726 ms	32 ms	2779 ms

TABLE III. PROCESSING TIME OF SLAMTMO (CASE 2)

	NDT SLAM	Scan data classification	Environment map update, moving-object tracking, and others	Total
Exp 1	1753 ms	242 ms	23 ms	2025 ms
Exp 2	1832 ms	285 ms	27 ms	2144 ms
Exp 3	1713 ms	239 ms	25 ms	1977 ms
Mean	1766 ms	255 ms	27 ms	2049 ms

In the experiments, LiDAR scan data are recorded, and SLAMTMO is executed offline by a computer. The specifications of the computer are as follows: Windows 10 Pro OS, Intel(R) Core (TM) i7-1065G7 @1.30GHz CPU, 16 GB RAM, and C++ software language. The point cloud library (PCL) [21] is used for NDT-based SLAM. Tables II and III show the processing time of SLAMTMO in cases 1 and 2, respectively.

Although long computational time is currently required, as shown in Tables II and III, the computational time can be reduced by optimizing the program code and using a graphical processing unit for real-time operations.

VII. CONCLUSIONS

This paper presented a SLAMTMO method in dynamic and GNSS-denied environments utilizing LiDAR attached to a helmet worn by a rider of micro-mobility (helmet-mounted LiDAR). To accurately perform environmental mapping and TMO, the distortion of scanning LiDAR data was corrected using the self-pose information by NDT-based SLAM and IMU information via EKF. Furthermore, static and moving scan data were classified by the EMS-based classification and occupancy grid-based methods. The performance of the presented method was examined through experiments in a road environment of our university campus.

Experiments in various sidewalk and roadway situations are now being carries out to thoroughly evaluate the proposed method. In future works, we will detect obstacles on road surfaces, such as curbs, gutters, and steps, using LiDAR and accelerometer to reduce the falling risk of micro-mobility. Additionally, we will include the obstacle information in the environment map.

REFERENCES

[1] E. Yurtsever, J. Lambert, A. Carballo, and K. Takeda, "A Survey of Autonomous Driving: Common Practices and Emerging Technologies," IEEE Access, vol. 8, pp. 58443–58469, 2020.

[2] N. Boysen, S. Fedtke, and S. Schwerdfeger, "Last-Mile Delivery Concepts: A Survey from an Operational Research Perspective," OR Spectrum, vol. 43, pp. 1–58, 2021.

[3] B. Huang, J. Zhao, and J. Liu, "A Survey of Simultaneous Localization and Mapping," eprint arXiv:1909.05214, 2019.

[4] S. Kuutti et al., "A Survey of the State-of-the-Art Localization Techniques and Their Potentials for Autonomous Vehicle Applications," IEEE Internet of Things Journal, vol.5, pp. 829–846, 2018.

[5] A. Mukhtar, L. Xia, and TB. Tang, "Vehicle Detection Techniques for Collision Avoidance Systems: A Review," IEEE Trans. on Intelligent Transportation Systems, vol. 16, pp. 2318–2338, 2015.

[6] E. Marti, J. Perez, MA. Miguel, and F. Garcia, "A Review of Sensor Technologies for Perception in Automated Driving," IEEE Intelligent Transportation Systems Magazine, pp. 94–108, 2019.

[7] S. Tanaka, C. Koshiro, M. Yamaji, M. Hashimoto, and K. Takahashi, "Point Cloud Mapping and Merging in GNSS-Denied and Dynamic Environments Using Only Onboard Scanning LiDAR," Int. J. on Advances in Systems and Measurements, vol. 13, pp. 275–288, 2020.

[8] K. Matsuo, A. Yoshida, M. Hashimoto, and K. Takahashi, "NDT Based Mapping Using Scanning Lidar Mounted on Motorcycle," Proc. of the Fifth Int. Conf. on Advances in Sensors, Actuators, Metering and Sensing, pp. 69–75, 2020.

[9] S. Sato, M. Hashimoto, M. Takita, K. Takagi, and T. Ogawa, "Multilayer Lidar-Based Pedestrian Tracking in Urban Environments," Proc. of IEEE Intelligent Vehicles Symp., pp. 849–854, 2010.

[10] S. Muro, I. Yoshida, M. Hashimoto, and K. Takahashi, "Moving-Object Tracking by Scanning LiDAR Mounted on Motorcycle Based on Dynamic Background Subtraction," Artificial Life and Robotics, vol. 26, issue 4, pp. 412–422, 2021.

[11] A.Yoshida, I. Yoshida, M. Hashimoto, and K. Takahashi, "Point-Cloud Mapping by Helmet-Mounted LiDAR Based on NDT SLAM," Proc. of 23rd IEEE Int. Conf. on Industrial Technology, 2022, to be presented.

[12] Y. Cai, S. Hackett, G., Ben, F. Alber, and S. Mel, "Heads-Up Lidar Imaging with Sensor Fusion," Electronic Imaging, The Engineering Reality of Virtual Reality 2020, pp. 338-1–338-7, 2020.

[13] B. Cinaz and H. Kenn, "Head SLAM - Simultaneous Localization and Mapping with Head-Mounted Inertial and Laser Range Sensors," Proc. of 12th IEEE Int. Symp. on Wearable Computers, 2008.

[14] H. Sadruddin, A. Mahmoud, and M. M. Atia, "Enhancing Body-Mounted LiDAR SLAM using an IMU-based Pedestrian Dead Reckoning (PDR) Model," Proc. of 2020 IEEE 63rd Int. Midwest Symp. on Circuits and Systems, 2020.

[15] E. Niforatos, I. Elhart, A. Fedosov, and M. Langheinrich, " s-Helmet: A Ski Helmet for Augmenting Peripheral Perception," Proc. of the 7th Augmented Human Int. Conf.,2016.

[16] A. Pangestu, M. N. Mohammed, S. Al-Zubaidi, S. H. K. Bahrain, and A. Jaenul, "An Internet of Things Toward a Novel Smart Helmet for Motorcycle: Review," AIP Conf. Proceedings 2320, 050026, 2021.

[17] T. Raj, F. H. Hashim, A. B. Huddin, M. F. Ibrahim, and A. Hussain, "A Survey on LiDAR Scanning Mechanisms," Electronics, 2020.

[18] P. Biber and W. Strasser, "The Normal Distributions Transform: A New Approach to Laser Scan Matching," Proc. of IEEE/RSJ Int. Conf. on Intelligent Robots and Systems, pp. 2743–2748, 2003.

[19] M. Hashimoto, S. Ogata, F. Oba, and T. Murayama, "A Laser Based Multi-Target Tracking for Mobile Robot," Intelligent Autonomous Systems 9, pp. 135–144, 2006.

[20] K. Tokorodani, M. Hashimoto, Y. Aihara, and K. Takahashi, "Point-Cloud Mapping Using Lidar Mounted on Two-Wheeled Vehicle Based on NDT Scan Matching," Proc. of the 16th Int. Conf. on Informatics in Control, Automation and Robotics, pp. 446–452, 2019.

[21] R. B. Rusu and S. Cousins, "3D is here: Point Cloud Library (PCL)," Proc. of 2011 IEEE Int. Conf. on Robotics and Automation, 2011.

Acoustic Emission Sensing of Materials and Structures

Irinela Chilibon*
*National Institute of Research and Development for Optoelectronics, INOE-2000
Magurele, Romania
E-mail: qilib@yahoo.com

Abstract—**Acoustic Emission (AE) sensing is used in the field for the testing of metal and composite, as non-destructive techniques. The AE technique allows to determine the size of the cracks, damages, fractures and failures into materials. Possible causes of the internal-structure changes are crack initiation and growth, crack opening and closure, dislocation movement, twinning, and phase transformation in monolithic materials and fibre breakage and fibre-matrix debonding in composites. Most of the sources of AEs are damage-related to the detection of these emissions. AE technology involves the use of ultrasonic transducers (20 kHz - 1 MHz) to listen for the sounds of failure occurring in materials and structures. The experimental works can determine practical information concerning the AE response of different materials and structures at mechanical strength and predict their behaviour and maximum strengths. As novelty, monitoring the stability of important construction structures, by AE technique makes possible to detect the onset and evolution of stress-induced cracks and prevent the structural failures.**

Keywords-Acoustic Emission (AE); Acoustic Emission technique (AET); non-destructive testing (NDT); Structural Health Monitoring (SHM).

I. INTRODUCTION

Acoustic Emission (AE) techniques have attracted attention to the diagnostic applications, material testing and study of deformation, fracture and corrosion, because they give an immediate indication of the response and behavior of materials under stresses, intimately connected with strength, damage, fracture and failure. AE technology involves the use of ultrasonic sensors (20 kHz - 1 MHz) to listen to the sounds of failure occurring in materials and structures [1].

The roughest localization method is guessing the source origin using the "first hit" technique. The sensor which detects an AE first defines a radius or a half sphere, respectively, in which the signal originated. For instance, this can be done for some cases in combination with other techniques or knowledge to "localize" the source of failures.

Fibre breakage, matrix cracking, and delaminating are three mechanisms that can produce AE signals when stress is applied to the material or structure.

The continuous research evolution in this field may be useful for a targeted diagnosis of the corrosion-induced damage severity and the recognition of corrosion sources through the AE online inspection and monitoring [2]. Also, integrated with additional information, such as metallography, AE technique can provide a valid tool for identifying specific features related to crack initiation and propagation mechanisms.

AE technology uses ultrasonic transducers in the frequency range (20 kHz - 1 MHz) to detect sounds emitted by defects that occur in materials and structures, which are subjected to mechanical pressure or temperature variations.

Determining the degree of degradation of mechanical properties and the residual life of metal structures under complex dynamic deformation demands has various applications related to bending, static and dynamic tensile loads and defect initiation processes [3].

In case of metal structures, fatigue failure occurs due to cyclic stress from operating conditions. The main mechanisms of failure occur from mechanical fatigue or thermal fatigue, such as: mechanical fatigue failure is due to cyclic stresses and thermal fatigue failure is due to cyclic temperature changes. The tipping point for failure is when the material fails at loads lower than the yield strength of the material. The acoustic emission as a monitoring tool has capabilities to detect fatigue crack initiation and propagation in mooring chains [4].

Structural Health Monitoring (SHM) allows the early detection of potential damages resulting from the natural deterioration of structural materials and the optimization of decisions over maintenance, repair, and reconstruction of the bridge asset [5].

The structure of this paper is organized as follow: Section II describes the Acoustic Emission sensors. Section III describes the Acoustic emission monitoring methods. The acknowledgement and conclusions close the article.

II. ACOUSTIC EMISSION SENSORS

The future market for electronic devices will focus on miniaturized flexible electronic devices with low power consumption. The development of piezoelectric films with excellent piezoelectric responses and low coercive voltages would therefore be advantageous [6]. Acoustic emission sensors are usual piezoelectric receiver transducer, having as active elements discs made by piezoceramic lead titanate zirconate (PZT), lead titanate (PT), barium titanate (BP) [7], PVDF materials, copolymers, and composites. Piezoelectric materials are among the most important new materials in this century because of their excellent performances.

Polyvinylidene fluoride (PVDF), also known as polyvinylidene difluoride and PVF2, is part of the fluoropolymers family, a group of specialised, versatile polymeric materials with distinct properties that result from the strong bond between their carbon atoms and fluorine atoms and the fluorine shielding of the carbon backbone. PVDF is a polymer with pyroelectric and piezoelectric properties and is used in the manufacturing of diverse high-purity, high-strength, and high-chemical-resistance products for applications in electrical, electronic, biomedical, construction, etc., PVDF has a similar structure to poly (tetrafluoro-ethylene) PTFE, except that the hydrogen atoms are only replaced by fluorine on every alternate carbon [8].

Piezoceramic-based AE sensors measure the acoustic emissions and are sensitive to the flexural wave motion (vertical motion to the surface). The acoustic emissions due to impact hammering, fatal failure, large disturbances, and glass fracture had a high-amplitude vertical component of wave motion, detected by AE sensors. Attempts were made to capture the in-plane component of the wave motion using fiber-Bragg grating sensors. Coupled piezoelectric film strain sensors, monolithic piezoceramic patches were used to measure the acoustic waves [9]. The schematic of the cross-section of a typical commercial AE sensor is shown in Figure 2. It has several components inside a steel housing. It has a backing plate, PZT material, electrodes, and damping material inside the housing. The top electrode of the PZT material is connected to the center conductor of the connector and the bottom electrode is grounded to the housing. A bonding agent is used to connect the AE sensor to the host structure [9]. Piezoelectric elements inside the sensor convert this pressure into current, which then converted to a voltage signal.

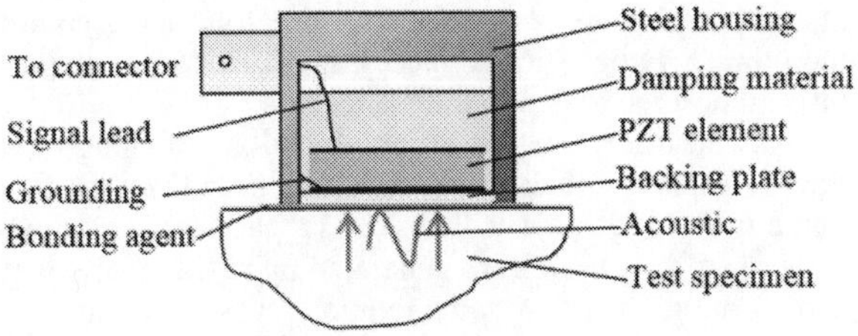

Figure 1. Cross-section of a typical commercial AE sensor which measures out-of-plane wave motion [9].

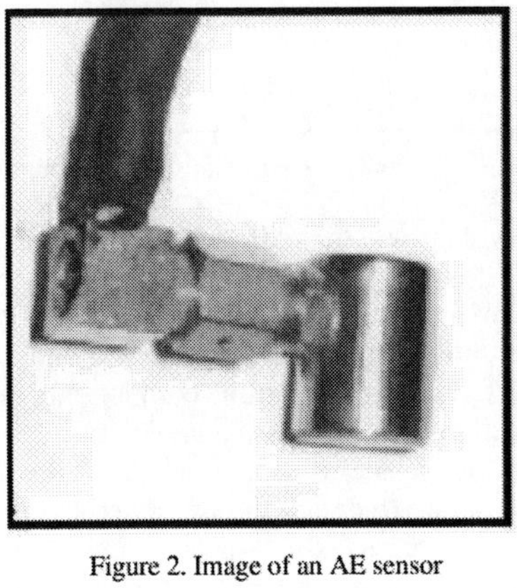

Figure 2. Image of an AE sensor

Figure 1 presents a cross-section of a typical commercial AE typical commercial AE sensor which measures out-of-plane wave motion [9], and Figure 2 is the image of a usual AE sensor.

Figure 3. AE sensor placed on a metal bar

As an application, a piezoceramic AE sensor was fixed on the surface of a metal bar by means of a silicone Vaseline-type coupling material (Figure 3), which ensures the maximum coupled transmission coefficient of the acoustic elastic waves at the piezoelectric element of the sensor.

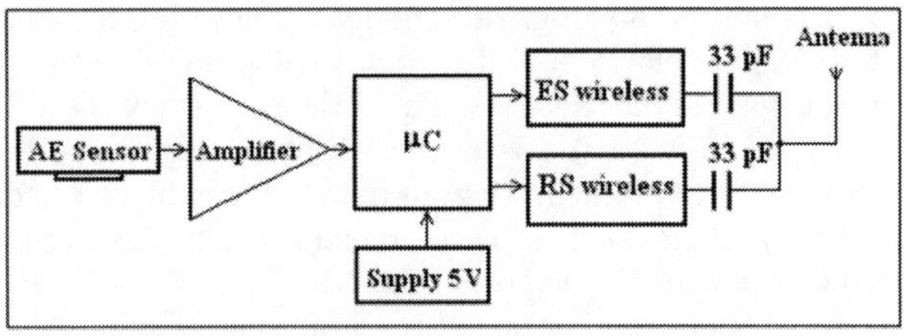

Figure 4. Block diagram of a module with acoustic emission sensor (SEA) [10].

More sophisticated devices were constructed as intelligent modules with AE sensor (SEA), used to pick up the acoustic emission signals. For example, an intelligent module with AE sensor (MSEA) is composed by: Acoustic emission sensor (SEA), Wireless transmitter (ES), Wireless receiver (RS), Stabilized voltage source with battery, Amplifier, PIC 18F452 microcontroller (µC) (Figure 4) [10].

III. ACOUSTIC EMMISION MONITORING METHODS

For historical buildings, Non-Destructive Evaluation (NDE) techniques are used for several purposes: (1) detecting hidden structural elements, such as floor structures, arches and piers; (2) determining masonry characteristics, mapping the heterogeneity of the materials used in the walls (e.g., use of different bricks during the life of a building); (3) evaluating the extent of the mechanical damage in cracked structures; (4) detecting voids and flaws; (5) determining moisture content and rising by capillary action; (6) detecting surface decay phenomena; and (7) evaluating the mechanical and physical properties of mortar and brick, or stone [11]. The choice of a technique for controlling and monitoring reinforced concrete or masonry structures is strictly correlated with the kind of structure to be analyzed and the data to be extracted.

A general approach for AE data analysis, which will be followed here is stepwise: (a) evaluating AE activity, e.g., the rate or cumulative number of selected AE hits or located events and noting their correlation with time or applied load; (b) evaluating AE intensity, e.g., the burst signal peak amplitude, burst signal energy, or continuous signal parameters and their behavior with load; (c) AE source location, if more than one AE sensor has been used, e.g., spatial or spatio-temporal clustering of AE event sources; and finally (d) looking for indications of different damage mechanisms, e.g., from AE intensity or waveform analysis [12].

Delamination behaviour of composites is a standard reference for all those researching laminated composites and using them in such diverse applications as microelectronics, aerospace, marine, automotive and civil engineering. In (AE) small amounts of elastic energy are released within a structure by a mechanical mechanism. Such energy release may arise from a variety of mechanisms, such as crack tip advance, plastic deformation, or other mechanical behaviour like friction and rubbing. This energy radiates from its point of release, known as the source, in all directions, propagating as an elastic wave [13]. The nature of this technique means that a source mechanism must be active (i.e. damage must be growing) in order for it to be detected, making it ideal for in-service structural health monitoring (SHM) and non-destructive testing (NDT).

AE monitoring appears to be a promising technique that can be used for bridge inspection to quantify the condition of steel-reinforced concrete, where corrosion is occurring, and where repair is needed.

Material study is another field of acoustic emission application. Particularly, acoustic emission is used for studies of:

- Environmental cracking including stress corrosion cracking, hydrogen embrittlement.
- Fatigue and creep crack growth.
- Material properties including material ductility or embrittlement, inclusions content.
- Plastic deformation development.
- Phase transformation, and many other.

Acoustic emission is a very versatile, non-invasive way to gather information about a material or structure. Acoustic Emission Testing (AET) can be applied to inspect and monitor pipelines, pressure vessels, storage tanks, bridges, aircraft, and bucket trucks, and a variety of composite and ceramic components. It is also used in process control applications such as monitoring welding processes. Acoustic Emission Testing is a non-destructive testing method that "listens" for transient elastic-waves generated due to a rapid release of strain energy caused by a structural alteration in a solid material.

Piping inspection is another common application, and Acoustic Emission is used efficiently and fast for detection of cracks, corrosion damage and leaks. There are multiple advantages of the method in case of piping inspection.

For example, in case of buried or insulated pipelines (Figure 5), there is no need to open the entire surface of the pipe but just a small opening for installation of sensors, while a distance between sensors can be from few meters to 100 meters. Acoustic emission testing is applied also for inspection of high pressure and temperature piping systems during their normal operation.

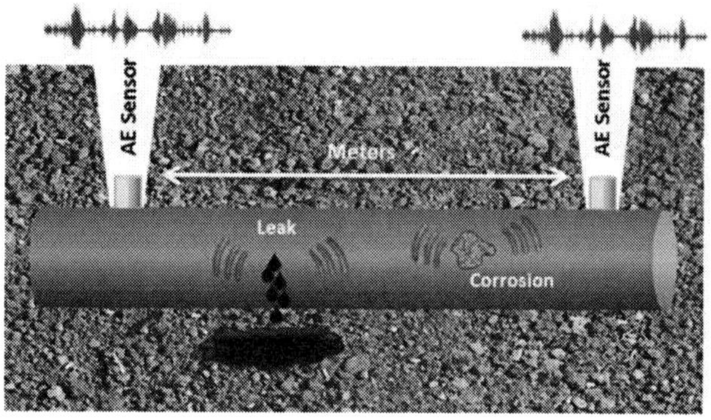

Figure 5. AE sources related to corrosion development and a leak in an underground pipeline.

As example, inspections of concrete and reinforced concrete bridges are applications where acoustic emission is used for detection of cracks, other concrete flaws, rebar corrosion, failure of cables and other. The method allows an overall inspection of a structure and long-term condition monitoring when it is necessary providing important information for bridge maintenance.

An elastic wave is a combination of longitudinal, transverse, and reflected waves, with a broadband frequency range from kHz to MHz. The AE is a phenomenon in which transient elastic waves are generated by rapid release waves, and a monitoring system requires a source and crack propagation or a tendon failure (Figure 6) [5].

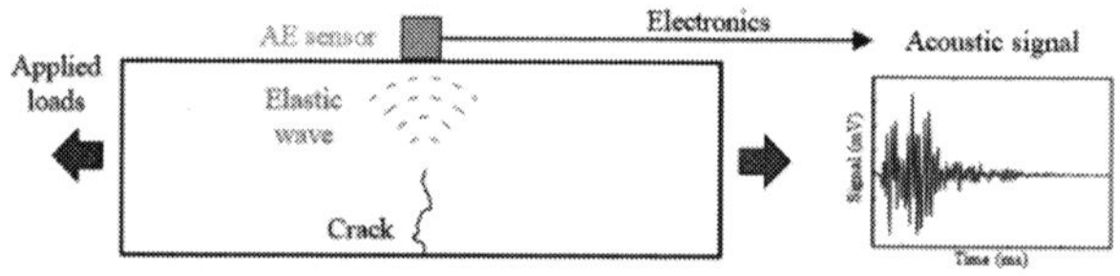

Figure 6. Working principle of an AE monitoring system [5].

The evaluation by AE monitoring of the complex mechanisms acting during stress corrosion crack (SCC) is still far from a clear, well accepted interpretation [2]. SCC is one of the most critical corrosion types and can also cause premature failures of structural components and should not be neglected in damage risk managements.

Monitoring a structure by means of the AE technique makes it possible to detect the onset and evolution of stress-induced cracks. Crack opening, in fact, is accompanied by the emission of elastic waves that propagate within the bulk of the material (Figure 7) [2].

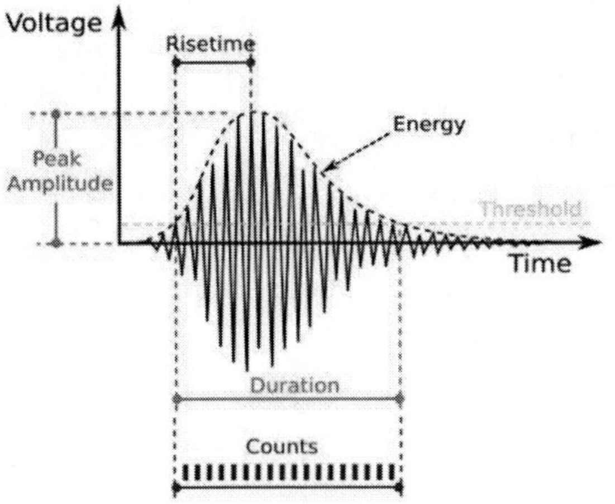

Figure 7. Schematic of an Acoustic Emission event and related parameters [2].

These waves can be captured and recorded by transducers applied to the surface of the structural elements [11]. The signal identified by the transducer (Figure 8) is preamplified and transformed into electric voltage; it is then filtered to eliminate unwanted frequencies, such as the vibrations caused by the mechanical instrumentation, which are generally lower than 100 kHz. In the Ring-Down Counting method, the signal is analyzed by a threshold measuring unit, which counts the oscillations exceeding a certain voltage value.

Non-destructive techniques were not accepted for long time for the testing bridges and other components of the infrastructures, because of inability of AE technique to determine the size of cracks [14].

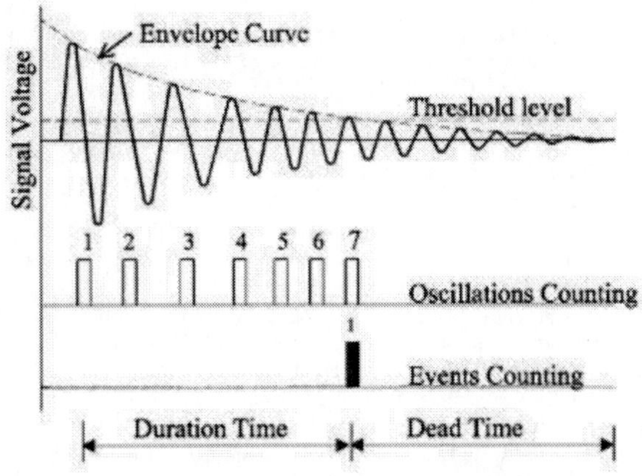

Figure 8. Counting methods in AE technique [11].

For example, one of the major issues in offshore equipment design is preventing the accumulation of fatigue damage over a long period of time. A full-scale fatigue test rig and the monitoring setup were arranged to perform the AE measurements [4]. The chain failure most likely occurs at the point of the intrados (the lower or inner curve of an arch) (KT point) and crown positions, due to higher localized stresses in these areas (Figure 9). Four sensors were used on links and a water-based couplant was used to facilitate the transmission of the sound signal between the transducer and the link's surface. Also, each sensor was equipped with an integrated 34 dB pre-amplification.

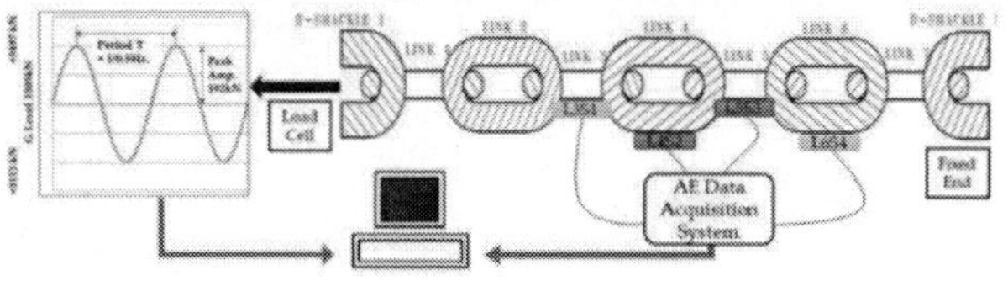

Figure 9. Test rig illustration: the chain is fixed at one end (right) and the loading (strain) is applied at the other end (left) [4].

After careful evaluation of the different AE signal features and all possible correlations, it appears that the frequency content of the AE signals is the most promising parameter. An increase of the average frequency is observed with the growth of the crack in the chain [4].

AE sensor manufacturers typically provide a sensitivity curve based on face-to-face calibration. This calibration procedure has been treated as proprietary information and described only inadequately. Calibration curves are usually in reference to the reference level of 1 V/μbar, but this reference remains undefined [15].

AE technique (AET) has found applications in monitoring the health of aerospace structures because sensors can be attached in easily accessed areas that are remotely located from damage prone sites. AET has been used in laboratory structural tests, as well as in flight test applications.

By signal graphic representation analysis in time and frequency can be determined the attenuation coefficient of the pulse into material. Figure 10 shows an aluminum pipe structure subjected to the mechanical stretching after its rupture [16].

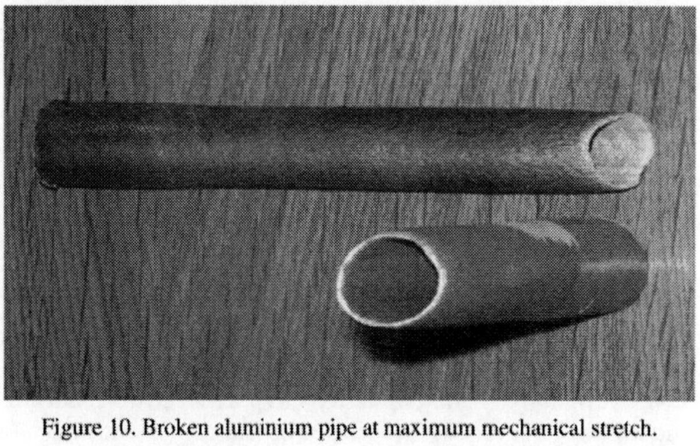

Figure 10. Broken aluminium pipe at maximum mechanical stretch.

Figure 11 presents prevailed AE signals by the sensor in the breaking moment of aluminium pipe at the maximum stretch. Therefore, one can detect these emissions and predict the moment of material failure, and causing damage to the overall structure.

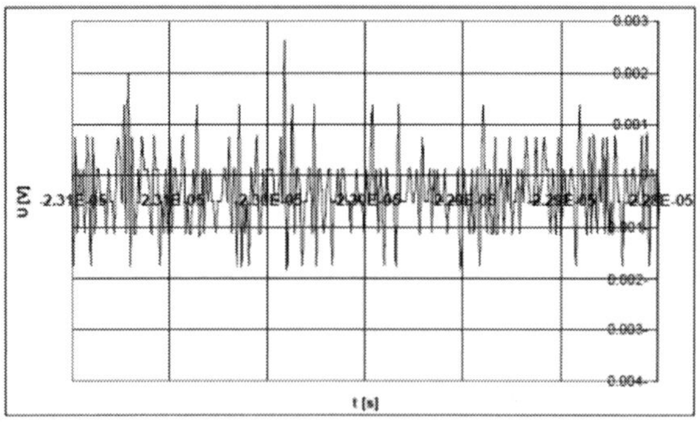

Figure 11. AE time spectrum for aluminium pipe (ϕ20x150 mm, and thickness 1 mm) subjected to the mechanical stretching [16].

The use of the phenomenon of acoustic emission during deformations of tension and bending makes it possible to predict the onset of critically dangerous states of loss of working capacity of metal structures.

IV. CONCLUSION

Monitoring structures by AE techniques could detect the onset and evolution of stress-induced cracks into materials (metals, non-metals, composites) and the crack opening is accompanied by the acoustic emission of elastic waves that propagate within the bulk of the materials and structures. These waves (AE) can be captured and recorded by transducers, type AE sensors, applied to the surface of the structural elements and provide the material behavior at mechanical stresses, fatigue and vibrations.

Crack initiation into material was determined by the appearance of the AE signal at low stretch stress levels. After the crack initiated, the AE signals around the zero stress were thought to be caused by crack-face grinding when the cracks were closed.

By these experimental works one can determine practical information concerning the strength of different type of materials, their mechanical limits at different stretch values. More, it can obtain practical information about AE of monitories complex construction structures, such as: bridges, containers fulfilled with liquids, etc., in order to prevent their possible breaking due to hostile environmental (shocks, long time vibrations, bending, temperature differences, etc.).

The internal stress redistribution of the materials caused by the changes in the internal structure can be predicted by the monitoring the acoustic emissions of the stress waves generated by the structures.

Possible causes of the internal-structure changes are crack initiation and growth, crack opening and closure, dislocation movement, twinning, and phase transformation in monolithic materials and fibre breakage. A number of challenges related to accurate localisation and classification of sources still remain, which must be addressed in order to exploit the full potential of the AE technique.

ACKNOWLEDGMENT

This work was supported by the Romanian Ministry of Research, Innovation and Digitalization (MRID), Core Program PN 18N/2019 and by the MRID through Program I – Development of the National R & D System, Subprogram 1.2-Institutional Performance-Projects for Excellence Financing in RDI, contract no. 18PFE/2021.

REFERENCES

[1] D. H. Kim, W. K. Lee, and S. W. Kim, "Analysis of Acoustic Emission Signal for the Detection of Defective Manufactures in Press Process," World Academy of Science, Engineering and Technology, vol. 53, pp. 1301-1305, 2009.

[2] L. Calabrese and E. Proverbio, "A Review on the Applications of Acoustic Emission Technique in the Study of Stress Corrosion Cracking," Corros. Mater. Degrad. vol. 2, pp. 1–30, 2021, https://doi.org/10.3390/cmd2010001.

[3] P. Louda, A. Sharko, and D. Stepanchikov, "An Acoustic Emission Method for Assessing the Degree of Degradation of Mechanical Properties and Residual Life of Metal Structures under Complex Dynamic Deformation Stresses," Materials, vol. 14, pp. 2090, 2021, https://doi.org/10.3390/ma14092090.

[4] Á. Angulo, et al. "Acoustic Emission Monitoring of Fatigue Crack Growth in Mooring Chains", Appl. Sci., vol. 9, pp. 2187, 2019; doi:10.3390/app9112187.

[5] D. Tonelli, M. Luchetta, F. Rossi, and P. Migliorino, "Structural Health Monitoring Based on Acoustic Emissions: Validation on a Prestressed Concrete Bridge Tested to Failure," Sensors, vol. 20, pp. 7272, 2020, doi:10.3390/s20247272.

[6] J-X. Chen, J-W Li, C-C. Cheng, and C-W. Chiu, "Piezoelectric Property Enhancement of PZT/Poly(vinylidenefluoride-***co***-trifluoroethylene) Hybrid Films for Flexible Piezoelectric Energy Harvesters," ACS Omega, vol. 7, pp. 793–803, 2022.

[7] R. Lay, G. S. Deijs, and J. Malmstrom, "The intrinsic piezoelectric properties of materials –a review with a focus on biological materials", RSC Adv., vol. 11, pp. 30657, 2021.

[8] J. E. Marshall, et al. "On the Solubility and Stability of Polyvinylidene Fluoride," Polymers, vol. 13, Issue 9, pp. 1354, 2021, https://doi.org/10.3390/polym13091354.

[9] Y. Bhuiyan, B. Lin, and V. Giurgiutiu, "Characterization of piezoelectric wafer active sensor for acoustic emission sensing," Ultrasonics, vol. 92, pp. 35-49, 2019.

[10] I. Chilibon, M. Mogildea, and G. Mogildea, "Wireless acoustic emission sensor device with microcontroller," Edited by: R. Walczak, J. Dziuban, Conference: 26th European Conference on Solid-State Transducers (Eurosensors), September 2012.

[11] A. Carpinteri, S. Invernizzi, and G. Lacidogna, "Historical brick-masonry subjected to double flat-jack test: Acoustic emissions and scale effects on cracking density," Construction and Building materials, vol. 23, Issue 8, pp. 2813-2820, August 2009.

[12] J. Bohse, "Acoustic emission characteristics of micro-failure processes in polymer blends and composites," Composites Science and Technology, vol. 60(8), pp. 1213–1226, 2000, doi:10.1016/S0266-3538(00)00060-9.

[13] K. M. Holford, M. J. Eaton, J. J. Hensman, R. Pullin, S. L. Evans, N. Dervilis, and K. Worden, "A new methodology for automating acoustic emission detection of metallic fatigue fractures in highly demanding aerospace environments: An overview," Progress in Aerospace Science, vol. 90, pp. 1-11, April 2017, https://doi.org/10.1016/j.paerosci.2016.11.003.

[14] S. Uppal, D. Yoshino, and H.I. Dunegang, "Using Acoustic Emission to Monitor Fatigue cracks on the Bridge at FAST," Technology Digest, February 2002.

[15] K. Ono, "Calibration Methods of Acoustic Emission Sensors," Materials, vol. 9(7), pp. 508, 2016, https://doi.org/10.3390/ma9070508.

[16] I. Chilibon, "Metallic Structures Behaviour under Mechanical Stretches" 17th International Congress on Sound and Vibration (ICSV17), pp. 1-5, July 2010.

Experimental Comparison of Vital Sign Extraction Using Off-The-Shelf MIMO FMCW Radar at Different Angles

Shahzad Ahmed, Junbyung Park, Chanwoo Choi, and Sung Ho Cho*
{shahzad1, jbp019, choi231121, dragon}@hanyang.ac.kr
(*Correspondence: Sung Ho Cho, dragon@hanyang.ac.kr)

Department of Electronic Engineering,
Hanyang University, Seoul
South Korea

Abstract—**Radar sensor provides a continuous and non-contact solution for human vital sign extraction. Radar sensor records the human chest vibrations and the received radar returns are processed to extract breathing rate (BR) and heart rate (HR). For directional radars, with an increase in angle of arrival (AOA), the strength of the signal reflected from target decreases. Since beamforming can increase the signal strength by steering the beam towards human target, this paper evaluates the performance of vital sign extraction with and without beamforming cases. Experiments were performed with human subject located at different AOA and vital signs were extracted in three different scenarios, which are (1) without beamforming, (2) with transmitter beamforming, and (3) with receiver beamforming. Preliminary comparison shows that focusing the radar signal towards the AOA decreases the mean absolute error (MAE) between the radar and the gold standard reference.**

Keywords-FMCW radar; beamforming; human vital sign extraction.

I. INTRODUCTION

Short-range millimeter wave radars have enabled several wireless sensing applications such as human behavior monitoring, gesture recognition and vital sign detection [1]. Radars were used only to detect large targets until 1970s when Lin [2] proved the feasibility of human and animal breathing rate detection using microwaves. Human vital sign measurement through radar has gained huge attention amongst the research community due to the fact that the abnormality in human vital sign can directly lead to several health related complications. Monitoring the patients and elderly persons continuously let the early diagnostics to avoid serious outcomes.

Unlike the other traditional Electrocardiogram (ECG) based vital sign monitoring, radar sensor provides a non-invasive and non-contact solution for continuous vital sign measurement [3]. The principle of vital sign detection works on detecting and processing the chest displacement with time. The acquired chest displacement signal is passed through a signal processing chain to extract breathing rate (BR) and heart rate (HR).

Off the shelf (OTS) radar sensors have a directional antenna which implies that as we move away from the center of radar beamwidth, the signal strength will decrease [4]. To overcome this loss, using beamforming concepts, multi-input multi-output (MIMO) radar are able to steer the beam towards the target under consideration [5]. However, the effectiveness of beamforming for vital sign extraction is yet to be explored. This study presents experimental comparison vital sign extraction with and without beamforming cases. For this purpose, we used an OTS frequency modulated continuous wave (FMCW) radar manufactured by Texas Instruments (TI IWR6843).

II. METHODOLOGY

In this paper, both transmitter (TX) and receiver (RX) side beamforming concepts are utilized while making comparison. To achieve high signal-to-noise ratio (SNR) using TX beamforming, the TX signals are aligned in such a way that the resulting constructive interference increases the TX signal energy in a particular direction. The TX system considered in this study comprises of horizontally aligned two TX channels as shown in Figure 1(a). Note that there must exist a phase difference of $\Delta\varphi$ between the transmitted signals $s_{t1}(t)$ and $s_{t2}(t)$ to achieve beamforming for a target at angle θ. The phase delay $\Delta\varphi$ is equivalent to the product of distance between two transmitters and the term $\sin(\theta)$ [5].

On the other hand, receiver beamforming is also achieved by delaying the received signal at each channel by a multiple of a phase difference $\Delta\phi$. The RX beamforming system with 4 RX channels is illustrated in Figure 1(b). In order to synchronize the phase of the received signal at each RX channel, the received signals $s_{r4}(t)$, $s_{r3}(t)$, and $s_{r2}(t)$ must be phase delayed by $3\Delta\phi$, $2\Delta\phi$, and $\Delta\phi$, respectively. The resultant vectors are added to achieve the RX beamforming.

Figure 2(a) shows the experimental setup for human vital sign detection. We considered five different angles. Vital signs with radar and the reference gold standard sensor are simultaneously extracted in three different scenarios: (1) without beamforming, (2) with TX beamforming, and (3) with RX beamforming. We used GDX-RB Respiration Belt and PSL-iECG2 Electrocardiogram Device as reference sensors to measure BR and HR, respectively. For robustness, three different participants were involved in the data acquisition process. Data from each participant were collected separately for all three aforementioned scenarios and mean absolute error (MAE) values between radar and reference sensors were computed. Figure 2(b) shows the OTS FMCW radar (TI IWR6843) used in the experiment.

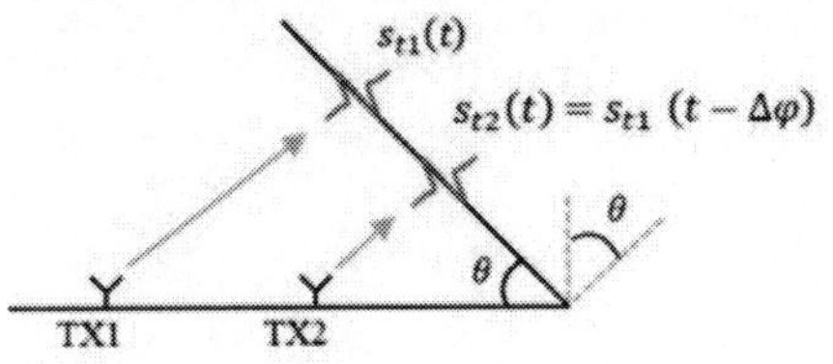

(a)

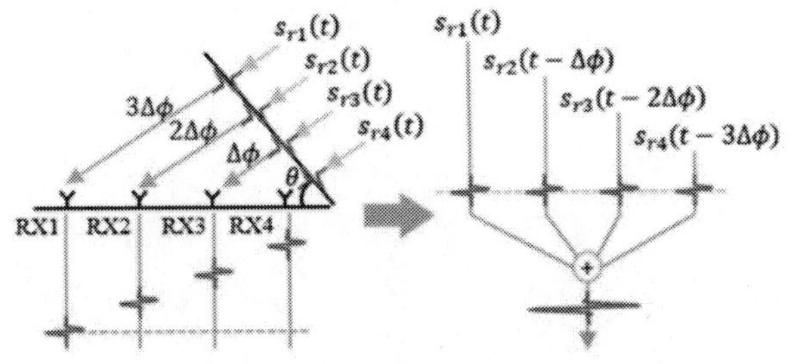

(b)

Figure 1. (a) TX beamforming and (b) RX beamforming considered in this paper.

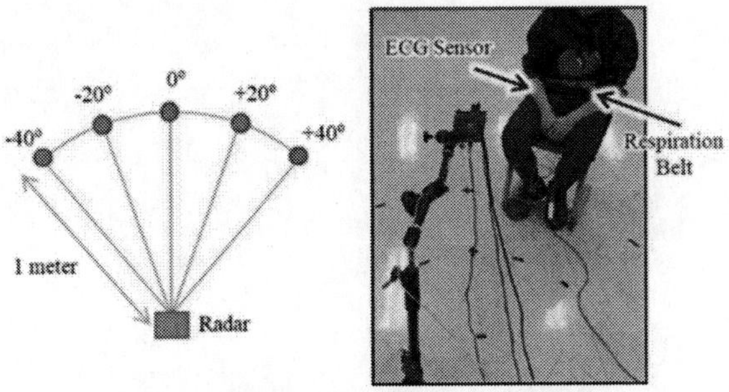

(a)

(b)

Figure 2. (a) Experimental setup to test vital sign at different angles and (b) the OTS FMCW radar (TI IWR6843) used in the experiment.

III. Results and Discussion

We compared the MAE between radar and reference sensor device in all the cases, and the results are summarized in Tables I and II for BR and HR respectively. Tables I and II suggest that the TX and the RX beamforming has slightly reduced the MAE of the HR mainly. Based on results gathered with OTS radar under consideration, HR seems to be the main beneficiary of beamforming. The MAE for the BR on the other hand is not decreased significantly in comparison to the HR. Hence, it can be concluded that for this particular OTS FMCW radar, beamforming can be deployed mainly for HR extraction whereas BR can be extracted without using beamforming. In addition, when the participant is in front of radar, beamforming does not increase the performance of HR extraction. In fact, Table II shows a slightly increased MAE for the case of zero degree.

In the future, we plan to extend the beamforming concept to extract vital signs for each of multiple humans coexisting at different distances and angles.

TABLE I. MAE Comparison for Breathing Rate

Angle (degree)	Without Beamforming	TX Beamforming	RX Beamforming
-40	0.71	0.73 (-2.3 %)	0.7 (1.4 %)
-20	0.33	0.33 (0 %)	0.36 (-0.1 %)
0	0.56	0.52 (7.1 %)	0.52 (7.1 %)
+20	0.77	0.54 (29.8 %)	0.44 (42.8 %)
+40	1	0.72 (28.0 %)	0.96 (4.0 %)

TABLE II. MAE Comparison for Heart Rate

Angle (degree)	Without Beamforming	TX Beamforming	RX Beamforming
-40	2.8	2.60 (7.1 %)	2.24 (20.0 %)
-20	2.40	1.69 (29.6 %)	1.71 (28.7 %)
0	1.12	1.51 (-34.0 %)	1.68 (-50.0 %)
+20	3.06	2.19 (28.4 %)	2.39 (21.8 %)
+40	2.23	1.85 (17.04 %)	1.60 (28.5 %)

Acknowledgment

This research was supported by National Research Foundation (NRF) of Korea (NRF-2022R1A2C2008783).

References

[1] S. Yoo, S. Ahmed, S. Kang, D. Hwang, J. Lee, J. Son, and S. H. Cho, "Radar recorded child vital sign public dataset and deep learning-based age group classification framework for vehicular application," Sensors, 21(7), 2412, pp. 1-16, 2021.

[2] C. Li, J. Lin, and Y. Xiao, "Robust overnight monitoring of human vital signs by a non-contact respiration and heartbeat detector," International Conference of the IEEE Engineering in Medicine and Biology Society, pp. 2235-2238, August 2006.

[3] B. Schleicher, I. Nasr, A. Trasser, and H. Schumacher, "IR-UWB radar demonstrator for ultra-fine movement detection and vital-sign monitoring," IEEE Transactions on Microwave Theory and Techniques, 61(5, 2), pp. 2076-2085, May 2013.

[4] S. M. Islam, O. Boric-Lubecke, and V. M. Lubekce, "Concurrent respiration monitoring of multiple subjects by phase-comparison monopulse radar using independent component analysis (ICA) with JADE algorithm and direction of arrival (DOA)," IEEE Access, Vol. 8, pp. 73558-73569, 2020.

[5] S. Sun, A. P. Petropulu, and H. V. Poor, "MIMO radar for advanced driver-assistance systems and autonomous driving: Advantages and challenges," IEEE Signal Processing Magazine, Vol. 37(4), pp. 98-117, 2020.

Fluorescence Assay for Spore Germination Detection

Fast Decontamination Assay

Andreas Tortschanoff, Sabine K. Lengger, Gerald Auböck, Cristina Consani
Sensors Division
Silicon Austria Labs
Villach, Austria
e-mail: andreas.tortschanoff@silicon-austria.com

Abstract—**Tracking viability of spores for assessing decontamination and sterilization quality is of utmost importance in medical and other clean environments. However, classical tests for spore contamination rely on bacterial growth, which is slow. Rather than monitoring bacterial growth, one can detect the spore germination process. Here, we present our method for reliable testing for spore germination by fluorescence detection of the associated DPA release. Extrapolating our results, we estimate that single spore detection will be possible with our method.**

Keywords – germination; time resolved fluorescence, component; spore detection; sterilization detection.

I. Introduction

Tracking viability of spores for assessing disinfection and sterilization quality is of uttermost importance in medical and other clean environments. Biological indicators, or spore tests, are the most accepted means to assess the sterilization process. They directly control the sterilization by exposing known highly resistant microorganisms and then controlling for residual bacterial growth, which is a slow process extending over several days [1].

Rather than monitoring bacterial growth, one could detect the germination process. We are developing a method for reliable testing for spore germination. During spore germination, dipicolinic acid (DPA) is released [2], which can be monitored by adding Tb^{3+}-ions to the solution and monitoring the fluorescence [3].

Here, we present details on our specific approach and first experimental results. Extrapolating our results to microfluidic systems, we estimate that single spore detection will be possible. In Section II the experiment is described and in Section III the results are presented and discussed.

II. Experimental

The measurement consists in the determination of the fluorescence from a Tb^{3+} complex formed with DPA. Terbium (Tb^{3+}) is chosen as it forms a complex with high fluorescence quantum yield [4].

For the investigated use case, we developed a laboratory setup based on time-resolved fluorescence collection as schematically shown in the inset of Figure 1. Briefly, UV pulses at 266 nm with a repetition rate of 18 Hz were used to excite the sample. The emitted fluorescence was collected orthogonally to the excitation by a large numerical aperture lens and refocused onto a Silicon photomultiplier (SiPM) with a 3x3 mm^2 active area (Ketek, PM3315-WB). No spectral filter was used in the detection path, to maximize the fluorescence collection. Instead, the signal was temporally resolved, which allows to filter out short-lived contributions from autofluorescence or scattered light.

Figure 1. shows fluorescence measurements for different concentrations of DPA. Signals start to saturate at ~500 nM. Concentrations below 50 nM can still be well quantified. These curves were used for calibration, in order to estimate DPA concentrations in the samples.

From different tests, the best conditions had to be determined, in order to provide favorable biochemical conditions for spore germination, which, on the other hand do not interfere with the fluorescence measurements. The indicator spores we used were *Geobacillus stearothermophilus* obtained from Merck.

The best results were achieved using 10 mM Trizma buffer, in part because its pH can be tuned to the value of 8.0, a commonly accepted optimum for the germination of spores of *Geobacillus stearothermophilus.*

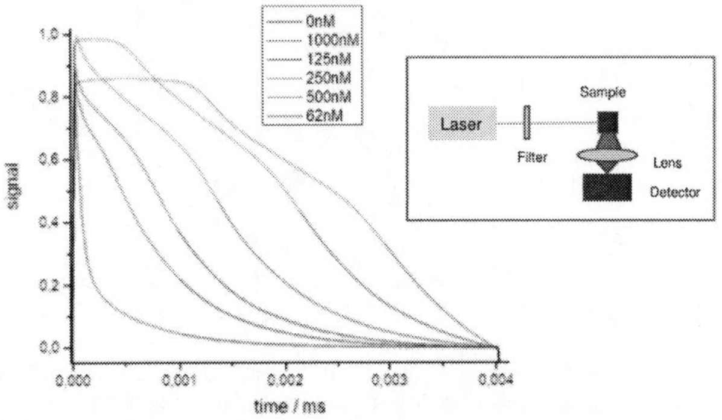

Figure 1. a) Fluorescence intensity of TbDPA in 10mM Trizma buffer for the DPA concentrations marked in the legend; Curves at high concentrations show detector saturation. (Inset shows a scheme of the fluorescence set-up)

Geobacillus stearothermophilus typically requires a relatively complex nutrient mixture for efficient growth [5]. Nevertheless, it was demonstrated that the early steps in the transition from a spore to a vegetative cell can be induced in simple media containing organic acids [6]. Here, incubation was conducted in a solution containing 1 mM L-valine solution at 65°C. Sterilization was done by exposure of the spore-samples to H_2O_2 over 45 minutes.

The overall measurement process is shown in Figure 2.

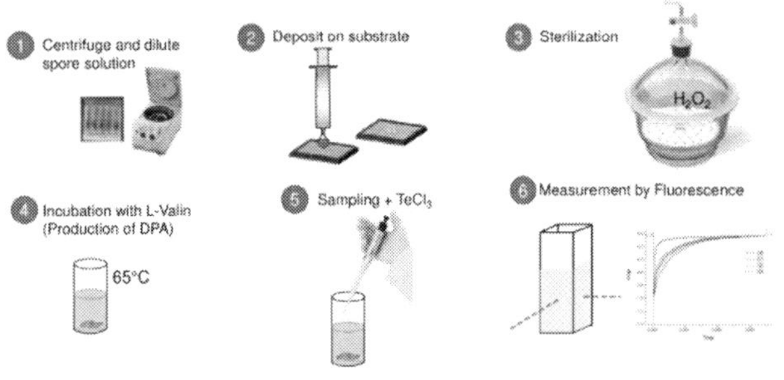

Figure 2. Process flow, as described in text

A spore solution (*Bacillus stearothermophilus,* Merck) was centrifuged, in order to remove residual DPA in the solution and then deposited on a substrate, which was exposed to H_2O_2 vapor for approximately one hour for sterilization. Subsequently the sample was dissolved in buffer solution (Tris, pH=8) and L-Valin was added to support germination. Germination was triggered by heating to 65°C and samples were taken after 30, 90, and 120 minutes of incubation. Flourescence decays were measured after adding $TbCl_3$.

III. Results and Discussion

Results showing the kinetics of germination are summarized in Figure 3. Spore solutions with 10^7, 10^6 and 10^5 CFT/ml were prepared and centrifuged for removing DPA from the solution. Germination was initiated by adding L-valine and heating to 65°C. Samples were taken at 0, 30, 90, and 120 minutes.

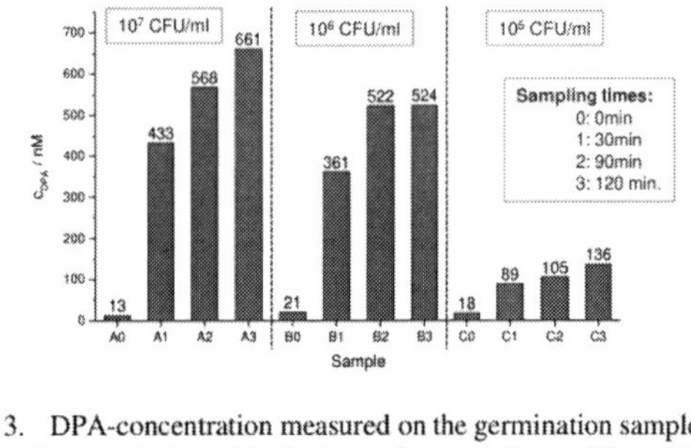

Figure 3. DPA-concentration measured on the germination samples. Sampling times are indicated in the inset. Concentrations of the original spore solutions were 10^7, 10^6, 10^5 CFT/ml for sample-series A, B, C, respectively. (Concentrations were estimated by comparing the measured fluorescence decays with calibrated samples like in Figure 1)

Estimating an average DPA content of 2.3 10^8 molecules per spore and assuming a fraction of 3% of DPA released by the spores [6], we estimate the concentration of DPA after germination of the spore suspension above (10^6 CFU/ml) of about 11 nM. Indeed, the jump in DPA concentration from germination can easily be measured and it is in the range of expected signal.

Extrapolating to the single spore regime, we would obtain a similar DPA concentration by confining the volume to the nanoliter. One spore confined to a single nl, would release a DPA amount of 12 attomol corresponding to an effective concentration of 11 nM within the small volume. Thus, single spore measurements are attainable in a microfluidic environement, where the spore and laser light are confined to a volume of 1 nanolitre, corresponding to channel dimensions in the order of 100 µm. This should be achievable in a micro-fluidic set-up combined with microscopic fluorescence detection. Further experiments will be necessary to get a better estimate about repeatability and measurement errors.

IV. Conclusions

Overall, we present first results from our approach of a rapid assay for spore germination detection, which can be used for sterilization validation. Using an optimized combination of germination conditions and a highly sensitive time-resolved fluorescence detection set-up based on pulsed laser excitation, we could determine the DPA, which is released during germination with nM sensitivity under realistic conditions.

We also estimated that single spore detection could be realistic, however, in order to reach sensitivities approaching the single spore regime, a microfluidic environment would be necessary.

Acknowledgment

This work was performed within the COMET Centre ASSIC - Austrian Smart Systems Integration Research Center, which is funded by BMK, BMDW, and the Austrian provinces of Carinthia and Styria. The COMET programme is run by FFG.

References

[1] P. Schneider et al., “Establishing a Minimum Incubation Time for Biological Indicators,” Pharmaceutical Technology, vol. 37, no. 12, 2013.

[2] A. A. Kolomenskii and H. A. Schuessler, „Raman spectra of dipicolinic acid in crystalline and liquid environments,” Spectrochimica Acta Part A: Molecular and Biomolecular Spectroscopy, vol. 61, no. 4, pp. 647-651, 2007.

[3] D. L. Rosen and S. Niles. "Chelation number of terbium dipicolinate: effects on photoluminescence lifetime and intensity," Applied Spectroscopy, vol. 55, no. 2, pp. 208-2016, 2001.

[4] J-C. G. Bünzli and C. Piguet., "Taking advantage of luminescent lanthanide ions," Chemical Society Reviews, vol. 34, no.12, pp. 1048-1077, 2005.

[5] M. Javed and B-Y. Namdar, "Nutritional optimization for anaerobic growth of Bacillus steaothermophilus LLD-16," Journal of Radiation Research and Applied Sciences, vol. 9, no. 2, pp. 170-179, 2016.

[6] T. Zhou et al., "Kinetics of germination of individual spores of Geobacillus stearothermophilus as measured by Raman spectroscopy and differential interference contrast microscopy," PloS one, vol. 8, no. 9, pp. e74987, 2016.

Towards Safety Methods for Unmanned Aerial Systems to achieve Fail-Safe or Fail-Operational Behaviour

Philipp Stelzer
Graz University of Technology
Graz, Austria
Email: stelzer@tugraz.at

Raphael Schermann
Graz University of Technology &
Infineon Technologies Austria AG
Graz, Austria
Email: raphael.schermann@infineon.com

Felix Warmer
Graz University of Technology
Graz, Austria
Email: warmer@tugraz.at

Hannes Winkler
Graz University of Technology
Graz, Austria
Email: hannes.winkler@tugraz.at

Georg Macher
Graz University of Technology
Graz, Austria
Email: georg.macher@tugraz.at

Christian Steger
Graz University of Technology
Graz, Austria
Email: steger@tugraz.at

***Abstract*—Drones and Unmanned Aerial Systems (UAS') in general are slowly taking over more and more areas of our everyday lives. They are already being used for cinematic productions, photography, structural inspections and will take over even more areas in the future like package delivery, surveillance tasks, or rescue missions. This inevitably leads to more and more UAS' occupying the airspace and therefore pose a danger to manned aviation, buildings, infrastructure, uninvolved persons, and other UAS'. In times of exponential growth of the Unmanned Aerial System (UAS) industry, the safety and security measures for UAS' becomes more and more significant. Until now, UAS safety has largely been the responsibility of the pilot, who had to take action if the UAS experienced any kind of failure. As the UAS industry continues to drift towards autonomy, the responsibility no longer lies with the pilot but instead, the UAS must have some sort of fall-back performance or fail-safe routine implemented. In our publication, we deal with such routines to establish fail-safe respectively fail-operational behaviour in case of sensor failure in an autonomously flying UAS beyond the visual line of sight of the UAS operator.**

Keywords–UAS; automated vehicles; safety; fail-operational; fail-safe

I. INTRODUCTION

Unmanned Aerial Systems (UAS') are already used in many cases and will be increasingly important for various missions and applications in the future [1], [2]. For example, in the rescue or localisation of earthquake victims [3]. Nowadays, UAS' are still remotely controlled in many cases, but in the future they should be able to fly autonomously to complete the missions without an operator. For this purpose, however, it is also important that these UAS' are equipped with appropriate safe and reliable systems. It must be possible to assume that a Unmanned Aerial System (UAS) can complete the mission with reduced functionality or at least establish a fail-safe status in the event of failures in the systems on board, such as a failure of an important sensor for environment perception. This requires implemented safety strategies in the UAS that it is able to be fail-operational or at least fail-safe. Research on safe and robust UAS' is already being carried out at a high level of intensity. The Airborne Data Collection on Resilient System Architectures (ADACORSA) [4] project, for example, whose representative cover image can be seen in the Figure 1, is concerned with resilient architectures for flight systems, among other things. The main vision of this project is to provide technologies to render drones as a safe and efficient component of the mobility mix, with differentiated, safe and reliable capabilities in extended Beyond Visual Line Of Sight (BVLOS) operations [4]. With this publication, we also want to contribute to the improvement of the safety of autonomous flying UAS' and to establish a fail-safe respectively fail-operational behaviour in UAS' in case of sensor failures. The remainder of the publication is structured as follows. An overview of background and related work is given in Section II. Subsequently, our novel methods and proposed solutions for the reaction to a sensor failure will be introduced in detail in Section III, and the achieved results, including a short discussion, will be provided in Section V. A summary and short discussion of the findings will conclude this publication in Section VI.

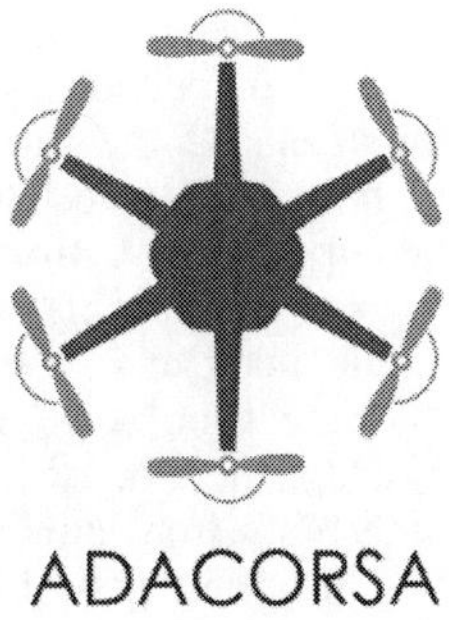

Figure 1. Airborne Data Collection on Resilient System Architectures [4].

II. BACKGROUND AND RELATED WORK

Safety, whether for automated vehicles to the ground or for automated UAS' in the air, is a very sensitive issue [5], [6]. Unlike manually operated vehicles, automated vehicles must be able to rely on the sensors for environment perception and on the processing units to a certain extent. For this purpose, established measures to increase safety are briefly discussed and terminology is defined in the following subsections. UAS' are then dealt with specifically. However, several drone projects, such as from Milhouse [7], have already been realised by using open-source software and off-the-shelf hardware - this is also our approach to evaluating our methods in this publication. Drones and other UAS have already been simulated for scientific purposes by Ma et al. [8] and Megalingam et al. [9], among others. Ebeid et al. [10], for instance, have given a general survey of open-source UAS flight controllers and flight simulators in their publication and highlighted their importance. A general overview of safety approaches and some State-of-the-Art safety measures in UAS' is given below. Furthermore, the role and use of a companion computer, which can assist a flight controller with complex tasks and provide further capabilities, will be discussed in more detail.

A. General Overview of Safety Approaches

To ensure safety, automated vehicles often rely on redundancy and diversity. Whether in aviation or in the automotive domain, similar concepts are applied with regard to diversity and redundancy. In detail, these concepts usually differ in the scope of execution [11]. A redundant approach relies on the use of several components of the same type. There can be various approaches how a faulty behaviour of a component can be detected or compensated. A diverse approach is similar. Here, however, different components are used instead of the same type. For example, in the case of environment perception, a sensor fusion of data from, e.g., Radio Detection And Ranging (RADAR) and camera is used. In a redundant sensor fusion approach, only data from similar RADARs could be used [12], [13], [14]. Depending on the constellation of the chosen approach, this leads to fail-safe or fail-operational behaviour [15]. The definitions of fail-safe and fail-operational are given below in order to clarify which properties are attributed to the respective behaviour:

1) Fail-Safe: In the event of an intolerable failure, the system is brought into a fail-safe status. The system differentiates between the unimpaired continuation of operation or a stop of the system. In case of a system stop, if the system has a transient error, the system is restarted. Otherwise, the system remains in stop state [15], [16]. In the case of a UAS, the UAS is of course not immediately stopped and brought down, but must be brought to a safe state, as described in Section III, for example.

2) Fail-Operational: In contrast, with fail-operational, an failure occurrence is tolerated and the system remains operational [15], [16]. In our publication, Section III also proposes a method for UAS' to achieve fail-operational behaviour.

B. State-of-the-Art Safety Measures for UAS'

Even though the use of highly automated UAS' is only just emerging, a lot of research has already been done to strengthen the environment perception and control of these systems. For example, Saxena et al. [17] have been working on learning failure responses for autonomous, vision-based flying of robust systems, and thus manage to learn simple failure recovery manoeuvres based on experience. Another approach that may also be interesting for UAS' is the introduced competence-aware path planning via introspective perception by Rabiee et al. [18]. This is a framework that integrates introspective perception into path planning to reduce robot navigation failures. Furthermore, research was also conducted on the robust control of UAS'. Vey and Lunze, for instance, dealt with an active, fault-tolerant control framework in their publication [19]. With this framework, it should be possible to ensure that the diagnostic result is always unambiguous from the point of view of control reconfiguration. Sharifi et al. [20] also dealt with fault-tolerant control of UAS' using a sliding mode control for a quadrotor UAS. This shows that safety measures for UAS' have also been dealt with in the recent past.

C. Companion Computers on UAS'

For safety tasks on UAS', so-called companion computers are also often used. But in theory, nothing more than a flight controller is needed for the UAS to be able to fly in terms of control devices. The flight controller is responsible for operating the hardware of the UAS, for example keeping the UAS permanently levelled and stable, and must not have any time delays as this would be fatal for the flight. Although the UAS could fly without any additional hardware, with just a State-of-the-Art and common flight controller, however, it would not be capable of handling any highly complex tasks [21]. An additional companion computer is used to perform difficult tasks, send commands to the flight controller and execute higher-level scripts. Another advantage of using a companion computer, like a Raspberry Pi, is that it provides an interface between the UAS itself and other hardware like environment perception sensors. In 2019 a new method for victim detection after disastrous events like earthquakes was published [3]. After such events, victims are usually buried under debris and can therefore not be detected by UAS' that use cameras for visual identification. The idea was, that a flight controller is connected to a Raspberry Pi, which in turn will be equipped with a microphone and a speaker. The UAS hovers above the debris and uses the speaker to draw the attention of the victims for them to know that someone is listening and that they have to make aware of themselves now. In case, the UAS records a scream for help it is going to be stored with the corresponding geographical coordinates and sent to the rescue teams. In this particular use case, the Raspberry Pi is needed to activate the speaker, record everything the microphone detects, filter out the permanent noise of the UAS, read out the data from the connected GPS module and send everything to a predefined receiver. All these things could not be accomplished with just a flight controller, but the portability of the Raspberry Pi makes it possible to perform all these complex operations on the UAS and forward only the final result [3]. The computing power of the Raspberry Pi allows also to mount a camera on the UAS and perform a precision landing based on real-time visual landing pad detection. The algorithm is executed on the Raspberry Pi, it receives a snapshot from the camera as input, processes the image, tries to find the landing pad, calculates the UAS's position and orientation according to the landing pad and sends manoeuvring commands to the flight controller via the serial port. Algorithms like this have achieved landing accuracy of up to 98.5% at a frame rate of approximately 13 Hz [22]. All the above-mentioned scenarios and functions prove that companion computers add further valuable capabilities to UAS'.

III. Novel Safety Methods for UAS'

In this section, three methods are proposed to achieve feasibility of preventing a crash of an autonomously flying UAS in the event of a sensor failure outside the pilot's Field of View. It is assumed that a faulty behaviour of the sensors can be detected by monitors of a companion computer on board of the UAS and thus the flight controller can be informed that the sensor concerned is no longer functioning reliably. In the simplest case, the UAS is equipped with four distance sensors, one on each side of the UAS. The worst case scenario would be if the sensor in the direction of flight would fail, as shown in Figure 2. The best case would be if the sensor in the opposite direction would fail. In the latter case, no immediate action would be required, as this sensor has virtually no effect on the UAS's airworthiness, under the condition that the UAS is not rotated. A reaction would be needed in case of a failure of one of the lateral sensors, but the required manoeuvre is the same as in the worst case, with only minor adjustments. During investigation, we came up with three different solutions on how the UAS should react in case of a sensor failure. The solutions are kept simple and straightforward, yet they are very effective and can even result in a fail-operational behaviour like completing the flight mission with a semi-functioning vehicle.

Figure 2. Simplified visualization of a sensor failure.

A. Fail-Safe and Fail-Operational Methods

In the following the three investigated safety methods for UAS' are presented.

1) Immediate Landing from UAS: The first approach we came up with is the most obvious one. In the event of a sensor failure, it does not matter which sensor fails, the UAS is simply landed right on the spot where the failure happened. A conceptual overview of this scenario is shown in Figure 3. This is the simplest solution but is not necessarily applicable at all times. For example, the failure could happen in a place where it is known nothing about the underlying surface, it could be a river where the UAS would be lost, or even worse, it could be right above a crowd of people where the rotating rotor blades of the UAS could cause serious injuries. If the UAS is used in a densely populated city, this solution would not be the first choice due to the potential risk of landing near people or in traffic. However, if the UAS is used for flights between cities over open countryside or in predefined areas, the UAS could simply land in the event of a failure to be accessible for quick repair of the sensor.

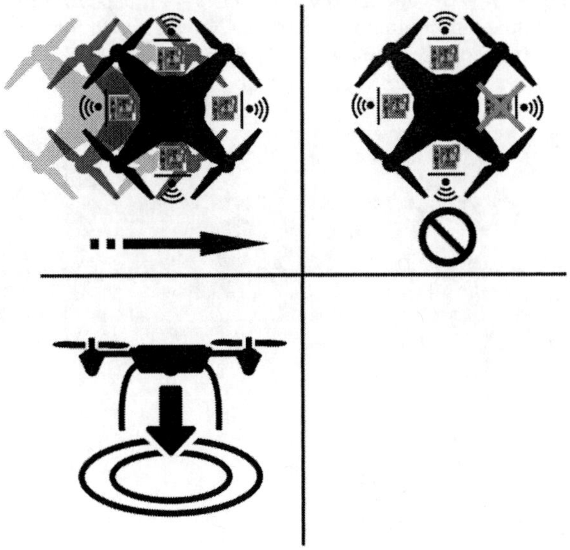

Figure 3. Immediately landing in case of sensor failure.

2) UAS Return to Launch Position: The second approach to handle a sensor failure is to return the UAS to its launch position where it started from. The applicability of this solution, like in the first one, is not always guaranteed, it works best if the sensor in direction of the flight crashes. In that case, it would not be necessary to rotate the UAS, if a lateral sensor crashes it would be necessary to turn the UAS around in order to be able to return safely to the launch position. In contrast to the option of simply landing, in this scenario, it is known everything about the condition of the landing site, since the UAS have already taken off from there. In addition, the UAS could fly back the exact same route it took on the way to the location of the failure. In that case, the UAS could be almost certain that the path should be free of obstacles unless there are other flying objects or moving parts involved. Figure 4 depicts this approach. Whether the use of this solution makes sense or not is also depending on the location of the sensor failure. In case, the event occurs shortly after the departure of the UAS, it clearly would be the first choice, since the UAS would not have to travel much distance to safe position. However, when the flight has progressed to the point where you are closer to the destination than to the take-off, it should be considered if a different solution would be more practical.

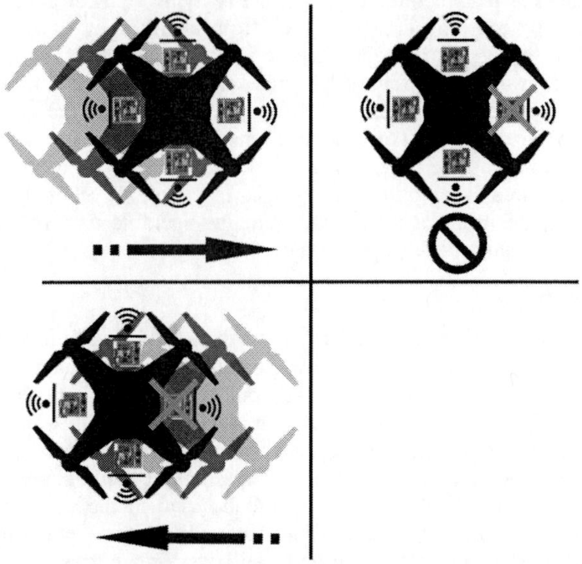

Figure 4. Return to launch position in case of sensor failure.

3) UAS Rotation: In the third and last approach investigated, the UAS is rotated in the event of a sensor failure. This approach is a temporary solution to maintain the airworthiness of the UAS in order to finish the already started mission. The idea is that depending on which sensor fails, the UAS is simply rotated to the position in which the failed sensor is looking backwards as seen in the direction of flight in Figure 5. The

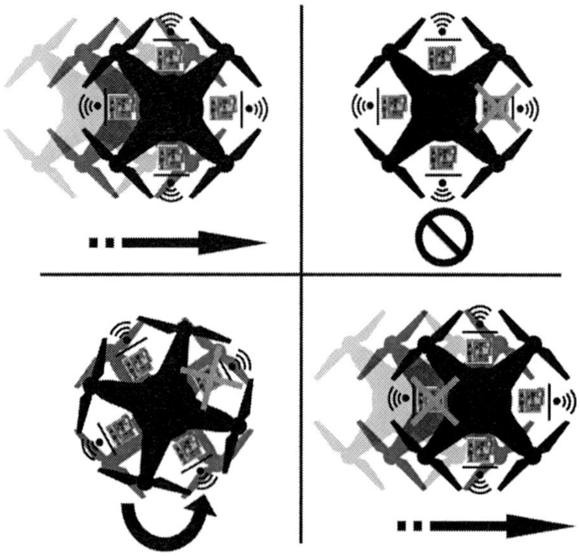

Figure 5. Rotate the UAS and finish the mission in case of sensor failure.

sensor opposite the direction of flight is not necessary most of the time, since we do not expect things or obstacles to approach the UAS from behind. If other UAS or flying vehicles get close to the according damaged UAS from behind they have their own sensors on board to become aware of the according UAS in their path. The remaining three sensors should be sufficient to complete the mission and land safely before the sensor can be replaced. This solution could be used in almost any situation, as the potential risk is kept as low as possible and thus there is no immediate danger to people or other things. With this approach, the UAS remains operable to a reduced extent, but still fail-operational.

B. Decision Graph for Method

In Figure 6, the decision flow during the mission of the UAS is depicted. It shows how the companion computer works from the definition of the way-points that the UAS should approach during the mission to a possible sensor failure and the corresponding fail-safe respectively fail-operational method or the successful completion of the mission. At the beginning, it is determined which method is to be used in the event of a sensor failure. Then the mission is started and it is continuously checked whether the sensor is still working correctly. This can be done by monitors, for example, which then notify the companion computer accordingly. As long as no sensor failure is detected, the mission can continue as usual. When the mission is completed, the mission stops and it is not checked for sensor failures until a new mission is started. However, if the mission is still in progress, it will be continuously checked for sensor failures and, in case of a sensor failure, the safety method defined at the beginning will be activated. When one of the two methods "Immediate Landing from UAS" and "UAS Return to Launch Position" are used, they are executed and the mission is stopped when the respective target position is reached. In case the method "UAS Rotation" has been

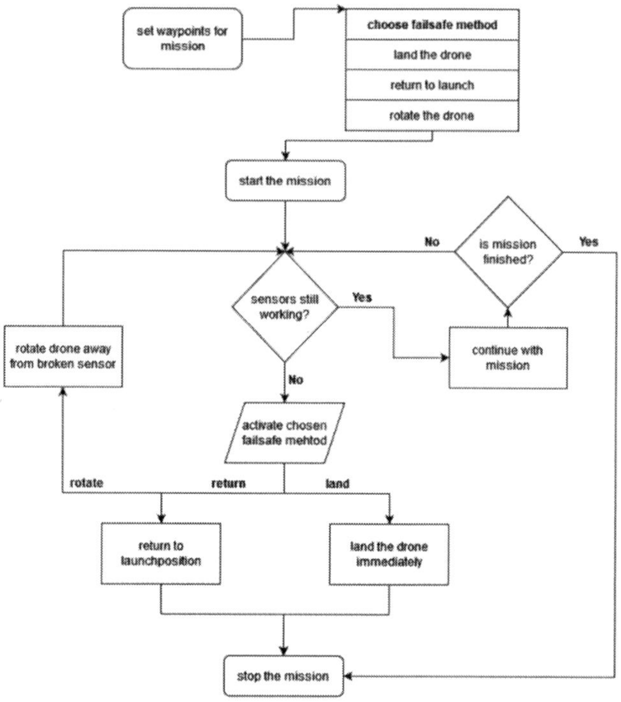

Figure 6. Decision graph of the companion computer for the three possible methods in the event of a sensor failure.

chosen, the UAS is first rotated so that a functioning sensor is positioned in front and the mission can then be continued. Here, the system will continue to check for sensor failures and if the current front sensor also fails, the method will be used again. Otherwise, the mission continues until it can be stopped.

IV. Setup of Development

In this section, the development and evaluation setup is presented. Since our intention was to investigate and test new methods to ensure safety, a corresponding concept of a development environment was designed. For this purpose, a UAS, in our case a drone, was simulated using open-source software and hardware, such as a Raspberry Pi [23] as companion computer, a Position2Go RADAR Sensor [24] from Infineon Technologies AG and a remote PC as GCS, as shown in Figure 7. The Raspberry Pi is the core of the

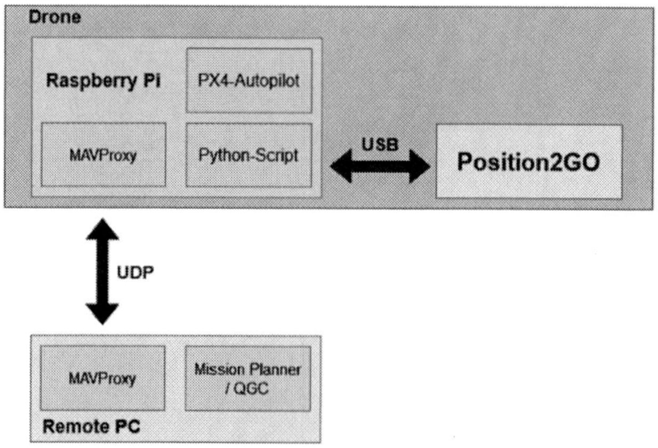

Figure 7. Concept of the development environment setup.

drone. It is running MAVProxy for the communication with the GCS, various Python scripts including the mission script and PX4 autopliot for operating the drone. The Postion2Go sensor is connected to the Raspberry Pi via USB. The mission script uses the Radar Host Communication Library for the status check of the Position2Go. The remote PC, the GCS, also runs MAVProxy and a Mission Planner/QGroundControl to track the progress of the mission in real time. The messages from MAVProxy are sent via UDP connection between the simulated drone and the remote PC. More detailed information on the hard- and software used is given in the following subsections.

A. *Hardware*

As already mentioned in Section II-C, a Raspberry Pi can be used as a companion computer. Due to the fact that we used a Raspberry Pi [23] and the Position2Go Development Kit [24] from Infineon Technologies AG as a RADAR sensor for our experiments, these two hardware components are described in more detail below. Although other hardware components - like the remote PC and a monitor - were also used, these two were the most essential to show that our fail-safe and fail-operational methods are relevant and essential for a companion computer for UAS'.

1) Raspberry Pi 4 Model B: For the experiments in this publication, the Raspberry Pi 4 Model B, depicted in Figure 8, was used. As with all earlier models in the Raspberry series, the operating system must be written onto a memory card. Due to the software used for our experiments, which is explained in more detail in Section IV-B, the choice of the operating system fell on a standard version of Ubuntu (Ubuntu 20.10, to be specific), which in contrast to Raspbian OS already has most of the used packages and libraries preinstalled. The

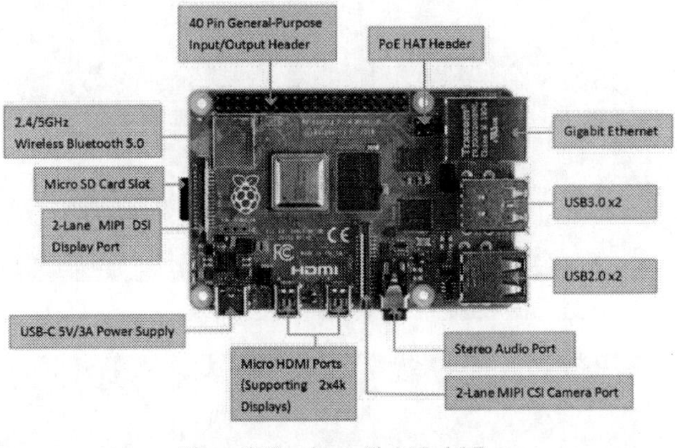

Figure 8. Raspberry Pi 4 Model B.

Raspberry Pi 4 Model B is far superior to its predecessors in terms of hardware. For this work the model with the following specifications was used [23]:

- Broadcom BCM2711, Quad core Cortex-A72 (ARM v8) 64-bit SoC @1.5GHz
- 4GB LPDDR4-3200 SDRAM
- 2.4GHz and 5.0GHz IEEE 802.11ac wireless, Bluetooth 5.0, BLE
- Gigabit Ethernet
- 2 USB 3.0 ports, 2 USB 2.0 ports
- 40 pin GPIO header
- 2 micro-HDMI ports (supporting two 4k displays)
- USB-C power supply (5V/3A)

2) Position2Go RADAR Sensor: The Position2Go RADAR sensor from Infineon Technologies AG, depicted in Figure 9, can be used to track multiple objects including humans, to detect angle and distance of moving and static targets, and to detect motion, speed, and direction of movement [24]. For

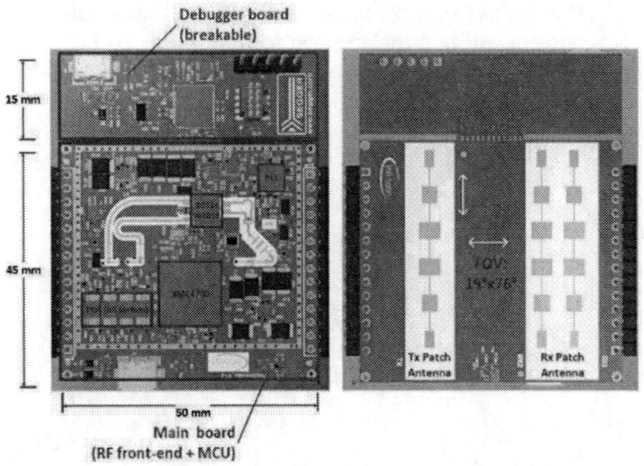

Figure 9. Position2Go board with main components and dimensions.

testing our methods, however, it is not relevant which sensor is used. In this publication, the focus is on the methods in the case of a sensor failure itself and not on how the sensor failure can be detected or what data is delivered. Another environmental perception sensor could also be used for this purpose. In our case, it is only important that we can inject a sensor failure in order to test whether our methods and whether they are applied correctly in the case of a sensor failure.

B. *Software*

In this section, the most important software parts that were used during our experiments are discussed. The focus is on open-source projects that are already well established for drones and UAS'.

1) MAVProxy: The originally intended use of MAVProxy was to operate as fully-functional Ground Control Station (GCS) [25]. It was designed as a minimalist, command line based software, which can be extended via add-on modules. Due to the light-weighted design and the portability to every commonly used operating system (Linux, Windows, OS X) it can run on almost every device, including smaller and less powerful ones like the Raspberry Pi. One feature is the ability to connect with other GCS, even if they are running on other devices in the same network or with the help of a VPN connection to devices outside the network.

2) PX4 Autopilot/Flight Controller: The PX4 autopilot [26] is an open-source project of the Dronecode Foundation, a US-based non-profit organization that also developed MAVLink (a communication protocol between companion computers like a Raspberry Pi, autopilots like the PX4 and GCS') and QGroundControl. The PX4 autopilot is basically a flight control software for operating UAS and other unmanned vehicles, such as rovers, fixed-wing aircraft, and many other experimental types, such as balloons and even boats and submarines. The software needed to build the autopilot can be found for free in a GitHub repository [26]. It is operating system independent and highly portable. After cloning the code to the device where the autopilot will run, it can be built the software by using the provided Makefile depending on the needed configuration. No specific hardware requirements have to be met, the jMAVSim simulator has to be used to simulate the UAS respectively drone. jMAVSim is already included in the source code, it has not to be installed.

3) Ground Control Station: A GCS is usually software that can be used to monitor and control the flights of UAS [27]. It

Figure 10. Screenshot from QGroundControl.

is typically linked to the vehicle via a wireless communication method but is running on a ground-based computer. On a virtual map displayed in the program, the user is able to define way-points for an autonomous mission. The user is also able to track the progress of the mission and check in on the real-time flight information like speed, altitude or distance to the next target through the program. A well known GCS is QGroundControl [28], which is developed by the same company as the PX4 autopilot. In Figure 10 a screenshot from the user interface of the QGroundControl is depicted.

V. Results

In this section, we provide the results of the implemented methods from our functionally safe system for UAS, which have been introduced in Section III.

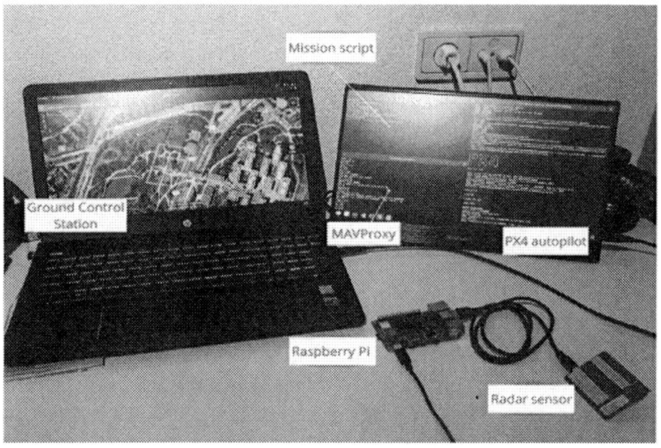

Figure 11. Evaluation and development environment setup in use.

A. Evaluation and Development Environment

The development environment used for this, according to the concept in Figure 7, was also used for the evaluation of the methods. The development and evaluation environment in use can be seen in Figure 11. The laptop (remote PC) is running the GCS, while everything on the right screen is running on the Raspberry Pi. Three different shells can be seen on the screen, one is running the PX4 autopilot, one is running the MAVProxy and one shell is running the mission script. In front of the remote PC, the Raspberry Pi can be seen, to which the Position2Go sensor is connected.

B. Method Examination

In the Figures 12, 13 and 14 parts of a single simulation run are depicted. The small window shows a shell running on the Raspberry Pi that outputs text-based information about the status of the mission. The map in the background is the GCS running on the remote PC to monitor the progress of the mission. The top red circle highlights the current output of the mission script to the Raspberry Pi, the leftmost circle shows the drone's orientation and position, and the bottom circle shows the drone's current altitude. The fall-back routine for this simulation run is described in Section III-A3, the drone will turn around in case of a failure. At the beginning, the system waits until a mission or a target position is known. This is shown in Figure 12. While waiting, the drone is on the ground. As soon as the drone receives a mission or a target position, it begins its flight. In order to check the required functionality of the predefined method, the Position2Go sensor

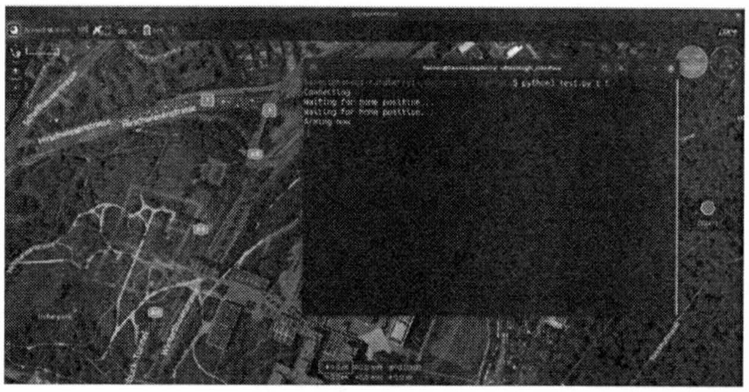

Figure 12. Drone on the ground at the beginning of the mission.

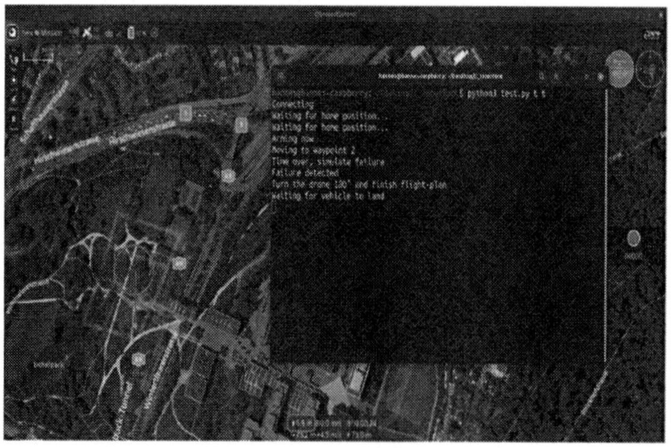

Figure 13. Drone in the air immediately after sensor failure.

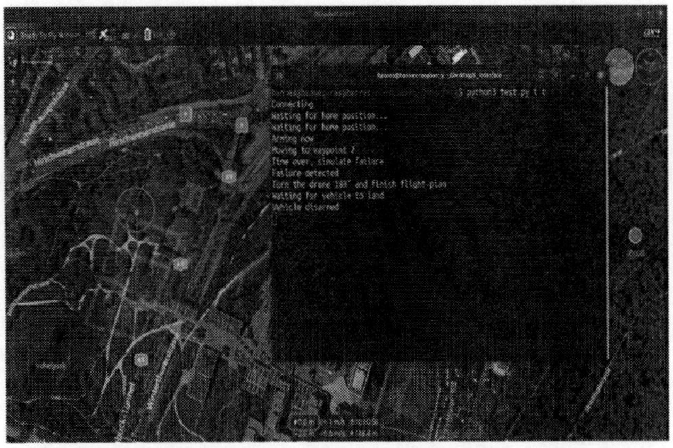

Figure 14. Rotated drone on the ground after the finished mission.

was unplugged during the simulation run and so a sensor failure was initiated. A monitor in the companion computer then detects that no more data from the sensor is arriving at the companion computer and reports a sensor fault. To detect more complex sensor faults, more sophisticated monitors must be used - but sensor fault detection was not the main focus here. However, in this case the predefined method was the "UAS rotation". Thus, in Figure 13 it can also be seen that the drone is already rotating immediately after the sensor failure. Figure 14 shows that the mission was successfully completed and the drone landed at the target point rotated 180°. If one of the two other methods is selected in advance, the simulation will run as described above in the event of a sensor failure. But in contrast to the drone rotation, the drone either lands immediately or flies back to the starting point and lands there. This depends on the chosen method at the beginning.

VI. CONCLUSION

As already mentioned in this publication, the research and development regarding UAS' becomes more and more important in our everyday lives and will play a major role in the future. We have discussed the given problem and presented possible solutions, in the form of investigated methods, for the scenario when a sensor fails during an ongoing mission. The simplest of them, landing immediately after sensor failure, has advantages, such as the low risk for other flying objects, but also has disadvantages like the requirement to fly over open terrain and to know the surface beneath. The second solution, returning to the launch position, is probably the least efficient solution of them all, as flying backwards with the remaining sensors is quite similar to the third solution. But with the third proposed solution, it is possible to finish the current mission. Despite that, depending on the location of the failure, the second solution is also worth to be considered. However, if strong wind or other influencing factors prevent rotation or make it impossible, the second solution must still be chosen. Considering the above, the most promising solution is probably the third and last one, where the UAS is rotated to the point where the broken sensor has the least impact on the flying behaviour of the UAS and finish the current mission. With this solution, the mission is not only finished, but also the risk of a partially uncontrolled landing for the people under the UAS or an abrupt change of direction for other flying objects in the immediate vicinity is avoided. Considering all of these aspects, the best solution for UAS' used in safety-critical applications would be a combination of all above mentioned options. However, the companion computer could either be developed in a manner that the operator of the UAS sets a fail-safe or fail-operational method when the UAS is launched, or that the UAS is developed to the point where it can apply one of the given solutions independently. This in turn would be more difficult, as the UAS would have to know everything of the surface beneath, other flying objects in the air, the already covered and remaining flight path, the task of the mission that is currently going on, and many other aspects. In conclusion, however, these methods can contribute to safe, highly automated UAS' for safety-critical applications in the future. Thus, safety in the immediate vicinity of such UAS' will also be ensured.

ACKNOWLEDGMENT

The authors would like to thank all national funding authorities and the ECSEL Joint Undertaking, which funded the ADACORSA project under the grant agreement number 876019.

ADACORSA is funded by the Austrian Federal Ministry of Transport, Innovation and Technology (BMVIT) under the program ICT of the Future between May 2020 and April 2023 (grant number 877585). More information: https://iktderzukunft.at/en/.

REFERENCES

[1] D. Bamburry, "Drones: Designed for product delivery," Design Management Review, vol. 26, no. 1, 2015, pp. 40–48.

[2] D. Câmara, "Cavalry to the rescue: Drones fleet to help rescuers operations over disasters scenarios," in 2014 IEEE Conference on Antenna Measurements & Applications (CAMA). IEEE, 2014, pp. 1–4.

[3] Y. Yamazaki, M. Tamaki, C. Premachandra, C. Perera, S. Sumathipala, and B. Sudantha, "Victim detection using UAV with on-board voice recognition system," in 2019 Third IEEE International Conference on Robotic Computing (IRC). IEEE, 2019, pp. 555–559.

[4] ADACORSA Project. Airborne Data Collection on Resilient System Architectures. https://www.adacorsa.eu. Retrieved: July, 2022.

[5] R. Altawy and A. M. Youssef, "Security, privacy, and safety aspects of civilian drones: A survey," ACM Transactions on Cyber-Physical Systems, vol. 1, no. 2, 2016, pp. 1–25.

[6] S. Riedmaier, T. Ponn, D. Ludwig, B. Schick, and F. Diermeyer, "Survey on scenario-based safety assessment of automated vehicles," IEEE access, vol. 8, 2020, pp. 87 456–87 477.

[7] M. O. Milhouse, "Framework for autonomous delivery drones," in Proceedings of the 4th Annual ACM Conference on Research in Information Technology, 2015, pp. 1–4.

[8] C. Ma, Y. Zhou, and Z. Li, "A New Simulation Environment Based on Airsim, ROS, and PX4 for Quadcopter Aircrafts," in 2020 6th International Conference on Control, Automation and Robotics (ICCAR). IEEE, 2020, pp. 486–490.

[9] R. K. Megalingam, D. V. Prithvi, N. C. S. Kumar, and V. Egumadiri, "Drone Stability Simulation Using ROS and Gazebo," in Advanced Computing and Intelligent Technologies. Springer, 2022, pp. 131–143.

[10] E. Ebeid, M. Skriver, K. H. Terkildsen, K. Jensen, and U. P. Schultz, "A survey of open-source UAV flight controllers and flight simulators," Microprocessors and Microsystems, vol. 61, 2018, pp. 11–20.

[11] V. Kharchenko, "Diversity for safety and security of embedded and cyber physical systems: Fundamentals review and industrial cases," in 2016 15th Biennial Baltic Electronics Conference (BEC). IEEE, 2016, pp. 17–26.

[12] J. Steinbaeck, C. Steger, G. Holweg, and N. Druml, "Next generation radar sensors in automotive sensor fusion systems," in 2017 Sensor Data Fusion: Trends, Solutions, Applications (SDF). IEEE, 2017, pp. 1–6.

[13] Y. Luo, A. K. Saberi, T. Bijlsma, J. J. Lukkien, and M. van den Brand, "An architecture pattern for safety critical automated driving applications: Design and analysis," in 2017 Annual IEEE International Systems Conference (SysCon). IEEE, 2017, pp. 1–7.

[14] A. Armoush, "Design patterns for safety-critical embedded systems," Ph.D. dissertation, RWTH Aachen University, 2010.

[15] A. Kohn, M. Käßmeyer, R. Schneider, A. Roger, C. Stellwag, and A. Herkersdorf, "Fail-operational in safety-related automotive multi-core systems," in 10th IEEE International Symposium on Industrial Embedded Systems (SIES). IEEE, 2015, pp. 1–4.

[16] P. Stelzer, A. Strasser, C. Steger, and N. Druml, "Fail-operational shock detection and correction of MEMS-based micro-scanning LiDAR systems," in 2020 IEEE Sensors Applications Symposium (SAS). IEEE, 2020, pp. 1–6.

[17] D. M. Saxena, V. Kurtz, and M. Hebert, "Learning robust failure response for autonomous vision based flight," in 2017 IEEE International Conference on Robotics and Automation (ICRA). IEEE, 2017, pp. 5824–5829.

[18] S. Rabiee, C. Basich, K. Wray, S. Zilberstein, and J. Biswas, "Competence-Aware Path Planning via Introspective Perception," IEEE Robotics and Automation Letters, 2022.

[19] D. Vey and J. Lunze, "Experimental evaluation of an active fault-tolerant control scheme for multirotor UAVs," in 2016 3rd conference on control and fault-tolerant systems (systol). IEEE, 2016, pp. 125–132.

[20] F. Sharifi, M. Mirzaei, B. W. Gordon, and Y. Zhang, "Fault tolerant control of a quadrotor UAV using sliding mode control," in 2010 conference on control and Fault-Tolerant Systems (SysTol). IEEE, 2010, pp. 239–244.

[21] V. Marojevic, I. Guvenc, M. Sichitiu, and R. Dutta, "An experimental research platform architecture for UAS communications and networking," in 2019 IEEE 90th Vehicular Technology Conference (VTC2019-Fall). IEEE, 2019, pp. 1–5.

[22] H. Jiaxin, G. Yanning, F. Zhen, and G. Yuqing, "Vision-based autonomous landing of unmanned aerial vehicles," in 2017 Chinese Automation Congress (CAC). IEEE, 2017, pp. 3464–3469.

[23] Raspberry Pi Foundation. Raspberry Pi 4 Model B. https://www.raspberrypi.com/products/raspberry-pi-4-model-b/specifications/. Retrieved: July, 2022.

[24] Infineon Technologies AG. Position2Go Development Kit. https://www.infineon.com/dgdl/Infineon-AN553_BGT24MTR12_XMC4700_Position2Go_DemoBoard-ApplicationNotesv01_03-EN.pdf?fileId=5546d4626cb27db2016d44631adb021f. Retrieved: July, 2022.

[25] ArduPilot Dev Team. Mavproxy documentation. https://ardupilot.org/mavproxy/. Retrieved: July, 2022.

[26] PX4 Dev Team. PX4 Autopilot: Open Source Autopilot for Drones. https://px4.io/. Retrieved: July, 2022.

[27] D. Perez, I. Maza, F. Caballero, D. Scarlatti, E. Casado, and A. Ollero, "A ground control station for a multi-uav surveillance system," Journal of Intelligent & Robotic Systems, vol. 69, no. 1, 2013, pp. 119–130.

[28] Dronecode Project. QGroundControl. http://qgroundcontrol.com/. Retrieved: July, 2022.

A High Purity Fused Silica (HPFS) Glass Substrate based 77 GHz 4 × 4 Butler Matrix for Automotive Radars

Ronak Sakhiya, Sazzadur Chowdhury
Department of Electrical and Computer Engineering
University of Windsor
Windsor, Ontario, Canada
e-mail: sakhiya@uwindsor.ca

Abstract— **This paper presents the design of a 77 GHz 4 × 4 Butler matrix on a High Purity Fused Silica (HPFS) glass substrate for automotive radar applications. The design and 3D Finite Element Method (FEM) simulation of the 4 × 4 Butler matrix beamformer has been conducted using an industry-standard CAD tool Advanced Design System (ADS) from Keysight™ Technologies. The 4 × 4 Butler matrix having a footprint area of 9.5 mm × 8.3 mm with 0.8-micrometer copper cladding thickness has been designed using a 0.2 mm thick HPFS glass as the microstrip dielectric substrate. The simulated insertion loss is –8 ± 2 dB. The return loss and isolation of the input ports are both below –20 dB respectively. This 4 × 4 Butler matrix can generate beam patterns at an elevation angle of –42°, –15°, 0°, 15°, and 42° when a corresponding port is excited. The maximum and minimum main lobe gain achieved are 20.322 dB and 16.763 dB respectively. These characteristics make the designed Butler matrix suitable for automotive radar applications, such as Adaptive Cruise Control (ACC), Collision Mitigation (CM), blind-spot detection, vehicle tracking, and pre-crash warning system.**

Keywords- Butler matrix; microstrip beamformer; antenna array; beam steering; 3D FEM simulations.

I. INTRODUCTION

The automotive radars have become the key enabling technology for Adaptive Cruise Control (ACC), autonomous driving, and Collision Mitigation (CM) applications for vehicles. Early automotive radars were designed to operate at 24 GHz center frequency. However, the narrow bandwidth of such radars was not suitable to achieve necessary range and velocity accuracies. Their large size made the system bulkier as well. Consequently, the automotive manufacturers focused on developing automotive radars operating at 76 GHz – 81 GHz frequency range to improve the range and velocity accuracies at a lower cost and smaller form factor following the regulations and recommendations of European Telecommunications Standard Institute (ETSI) and Federal Communications Commission (FCC) [1], [2]. Additionally, as the millimeter waves at high frequencies undergo very less absorption in human tissues due to their lower penetration through the human skin [3], the 76 GHz – 81 GHz is safer compared to 24 GHz.

In any communication system, it is necessary to adjust the antenna beams in appropriate directions so that the electromagnetic signals are transmitted and received between the end users with minimum signal loss. Modern communication systems consist of multibeam array antennas which are typically backed by Radio Frequency (RF) beamformers to achieve the target of beam steering with wide angle coverage [4]. There are several RF beamformers, such as Butler matrix [5], Rotman lens [6], [7], Blass matrix [8] and Nolen matrix [9], [10]. Out of all these, the advantages of Butler matrix forces to be an ideal candidate in terms of size, manufacturing costs, bandwidth, reliability, and reciprocity; therefore, it is widely used in several applications such as Internet of Things (IoT), Wi-Fi, base station, satellite communications as well as automotive radars [11]–[19].

The authors in [4] presented an excellent comprehensive analysis of available Butler matrices to conclude that a bilayer Butler matrix designed using meta-material substrate-based transmission lines is more suitable for 5G applications. However, the design and fabrication of transmission lines with meta-material substrates for each component of the Butler matrix is complex and demand further technological advances.

In [19], the design and fabrication of a 77 GHz planar Butler matrix implemented using a Substrate Integrated Waveguide (SIW) technology has been presented. However, the fabrication of the device is complex as the implementation requires several metal vias to direct the propagation of electromagnetic signals to realize the beamforming and beam steering capability.

Investigation by the authors of this paper show that as the microstrip transmission lines are comparatively easier to design and fabricate, the design and fabrication complexity of SIW based Butler matrix can be minimized by realizing an appropriate geometry microstrip Butler matrix with necessary input and output ports to achieve desired spatial resolutions. Due to easier small form factor fabrication of such microstrip Butler matrices, they can be easily integrated to realize small form factor simpler but superior functionality automotive radars.

Microstrip technology involves use of an appropriate substrate sandwiched between a conducting layer and a ground layer. The authors in [20], [21] recommended that glass substrates are better suited for W-band applications due to their superior performance compared to organic and ceramic substrates in terms of reliability, surface roughness, loss tangent, thickness, dimensional and thermal stability. Accordingly, a HPFS glass substrate from Corning™ has been selected as the substrate material to design the target 77 GHz center frequency 4 × 4 microstrip Butler matrix. The selected substrate has a low loss tangent (tan δ) of 0.0005, surface roughness < 10 Å, and a dielectric constant (ε_r) of 3.82 at 77 GHz [22], [23].

In this context, this paper presents the design and simulation results of a HPFS glass substrate-based 77 GHz 4 × 4 microstrip Butler matrix. The rest of the paper has been organized in the following manner: Section 1 describes the state-of-the-art of available Butler matrices and its need to be used in automotive radars. In Section 2, the theory and working principle of Butler matrix is described followed by the design and results of microstrip components and complete 4 × 4 Butler matrix. The beamforming capability of the designed 4 × 4 Butler matrix is also displayed. Section 3 and 4 describes the conclusion and acknowledgement followed by references section.

II. MICROSTRIP BUTLER MATRIX DESIGN

The Butler matrix is a passive beamforming network having N input ports (beam ports) and N output ports, where $N = 2^n$ and n is a positive non-zero integer. Each input port is connected to all output ports with high isolation between input ports. During operation, an RF signal is fed at one of the input ports. The corresponding signals received at the output ports are fed to an antenna array such that the phase difference among the antenna array elements remains the same. The block diagram of a 4 × 4 Butler matrix composed of 90° hybrid couplers, crossovers, and 45° phase shifters is shown in Figure 1.

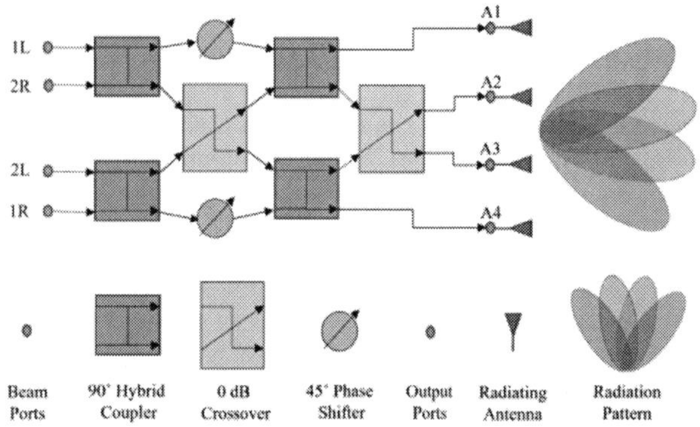

Figure 1. Beamforming by 4 × 4 Butler matrix.

In Figure 1, the Butler matrix is feeding a four-element linear antenna array. The detailed theories of operation a Butler matrix are available in [4], [5], [11]–[18].

The operational phase parameters of the 4 × 4 Butler matrix in Figure 1 are provided in Table I. The radiation patterns are observed at a constant azimuthal angle (φ) = 90°. The equations to determine values of phase difference (Δϕ) and beam angle (θ) are available in [18].

The design challenge is to determine the optimized dimensions of the HPFS glass substrate-based 77 GHz microstrip transmissions lines to realize the 90° hybrid couplers, crossovers, and 45° phase shifters.

TABLE I PHASE DISTRIBUTION IN 4 × 4 BUTLER MATRIX

	Beam Ports			
Output ports	**1L**	**2R**	**2L**	**1R**
A1	−45	−135	−90	−180
A2	−90	0/360	−225/135	−135
A3	−135	−225/135	0/360	−90
A4	−180	−90	−135	−45
Phase difference (Δϕ)	45	−135	135	−45
Beam angle (θ)	−14.47	48.6	−48.6	14.47

*All values are in degrees.

It was found through simulation studies by the authors that the microstrip width at the port terminals must be between 0.1 mm and 0.2 mm to excite the 77 GHz RF signals into the Butler matrix network with minimum return loss. The characteristic impedance of microstrip lines in the Butler matrix needs to be within 70 Ω and 100 Ω.

A. 90° Hybrid Coupler

The 90° hybrid coupler is a four-port directional coupler which is used to divide the input power equally at respective output ports and provide 90° phase difference across the output ports. Figure 2 shows the layout of the designed 90° hybrid coupler at 77 GHz in ADS. The corresponding widths and lengths are found by repetitive parametric optimization techniques in ADS and are listed in Table II.

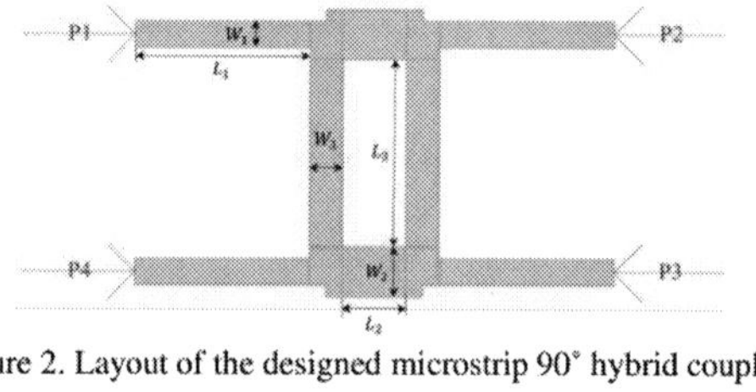

Figure 2. Layout of the designed microstrip 90° hybrid coupler.

TABLE II DIMENSIONS OF DESIGNED MICROSTRIP 90 HYBRID COUPLER

Parameter	W_1	L_1	W_2	L_2	W_3	L_3
Values(mm)	0.118	0.779	0.145	0.816	0.22	0.28

*All values are in mm.

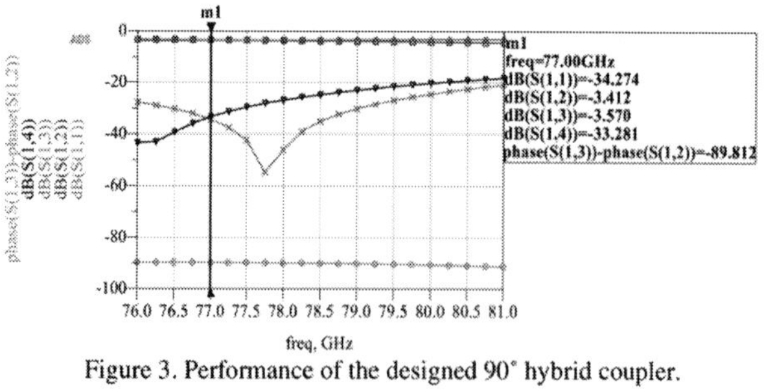

Figure 3. Performance of the designed 90° hybrid coupler.

The 3D FEM simulation results of the 90° hybrid coupler at 77 GHz frequency are shown in Figure 3. The phase shift between the output signals at port 2 and 3 of the 90° hybrid coupler is 89.812 degrees. The simulated insertion loss between port 1 and port 2 is –3.412 dB and that between port 1 and port 3 is –3.57 dB. The return loss is –34.274 dB and isolation of port 1 and port 4 or port 2 and port 3 is –33.281 dB.

B. Crossover

A crossover is also a directional coupler used to spatially switch a signal in a planar geometry without any coupling. The typical design of a microstrip crossover involves the cascading two 90° hybrid couplers. However, as per the design requirements of 4 × 4 Butler matrix, the design of 0 dB crossover was modified by connection of 90° curved bends at each port and optimized in ADS using 3D FEM simulations to get ideally 0 dB crossover. Figure 4 shows the layout of the designed microstrip crossover.

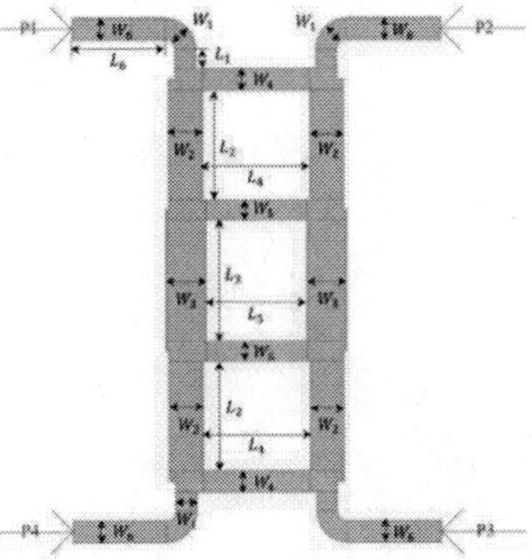

Figure 4. Layout of the designed crossover.

The corresponding values of widths and lengths of crossover are provided in Table III. These values are found by repetitive iterations of parametric optimization techniques in ADS.

TABLE III DIMENSIONS OF DESIGNED CROSSOVER.

Parameters	W_1	W_2	W_3	W_4	W_5	W_6
Values(mm)	0.116	0.192	0.226	0.12	0.11	0.122

Parameters	L_1	L_2	L_3	L_4	L_5	L_6
Values(mm)	0.107	0.618	0.686	0.616	0.582	0.547

*All values are in mm.

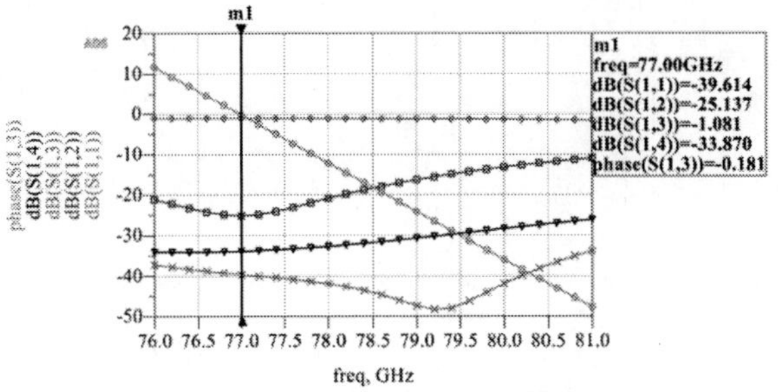

Figure 5. Performance of the designed crossover.

The performance values of the designed crossover shown in Figure 5 are optimum at frequency of 77 GHz. The isolation of port 1 and port 4 is –33.87 dB and that for port 1 and port 2 is –25.137 dB. The corresponding return loss is –39.614 dB. The insertion loss and phase shift between port 1 and port 3 is –1.081 dB and –0.181°.

C. 45° Phase Shifter

The implemented phase shifter is a microstrip transmission line that is used to adjust the phases of the output signals of the various components in the Butler matrix. To obtain the phase distribution as listed in Table I, it is necessary to design 45° phase shifters.

The 45° phase shifter as shown in Figure 6 was designed by optimizing the distance between the ports P1 and P2 and then tuning the length L_2. The corresponding values of width and lengths are given in Table IV.

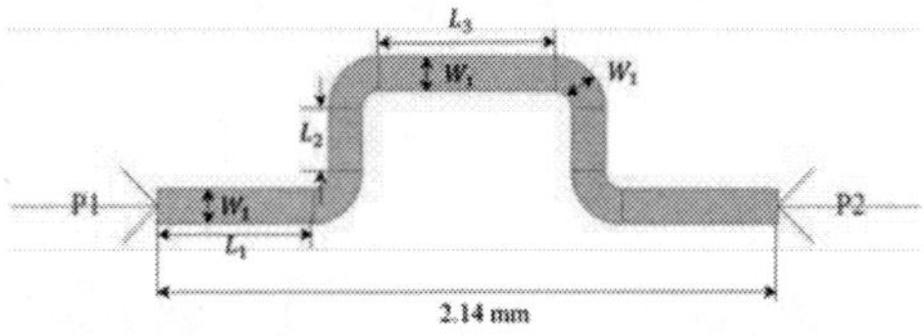

Figure 6. Layout of the designed 45° phase shifter.

TABLE IV. DIMENSIONS OF DESIGNED 45° PHASE SHIFTER.

Parameter	W_1	L_1	L_2	L_3
Values(mm)	0.118	0.532	0.136	0.616

*All values are in mm.

The performance of the designed 45° phase shifter is shown in Figure 7. The insertion loss and phase difference between the input port and output port at 77 GHz frequency are –0.156 dB and –45° respectively.

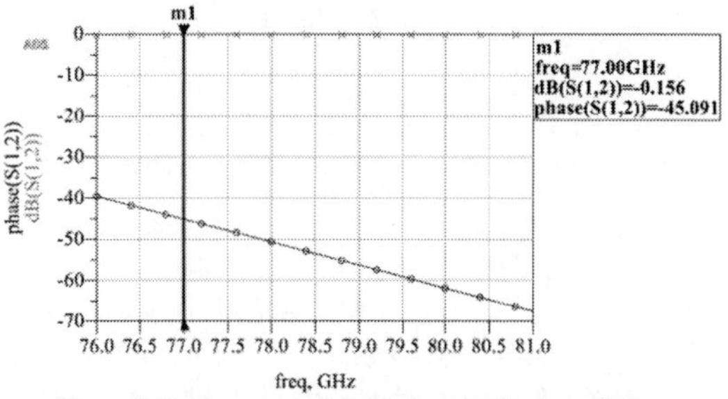

Figure 7. Performance of the designed 45° phase shifter.

D. 4 × 4 Butler Matrix S-parameter Simulation

After successfully optimizing the designs of 90° hybrid coupler, crossover, and 45° phase shifter, the components were then integrated as per the block diagram shown in Figure 1 to realize the complete 4 × 4 Butler matrix as shown in Figure 8. The beam ports 1L, 2R, 2L, and 1R are the same as P1, P2, P3, and P4 respectively. The total footprint area of the completed 4 × 4 Butler matrix is 9.5 mm × 8.3 mm. Figure 9 shows the S-parameters of the designed Butler matrix in ADS obtained through 3D FEM simulations.

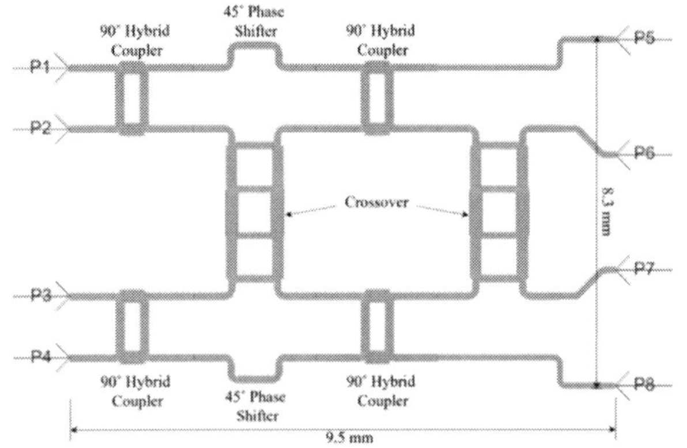

Figure 8. Layout of the complete 4 × 4 Butler matrix.

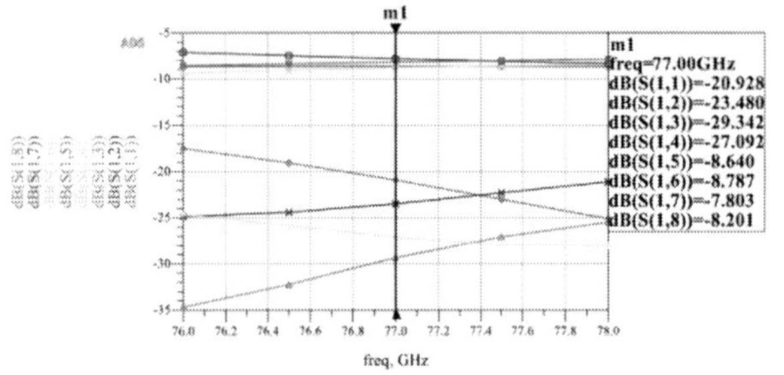

(a)

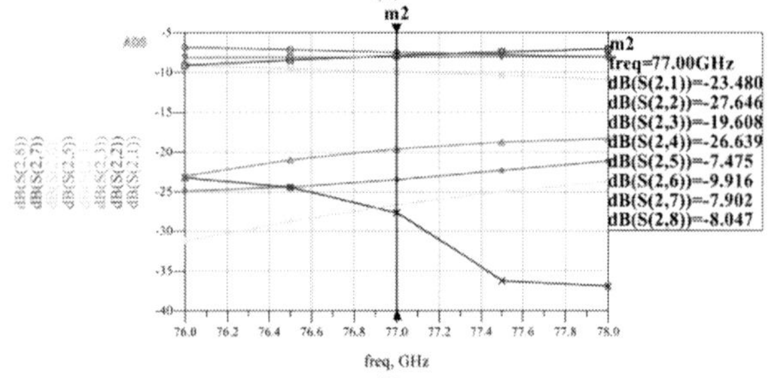

(b)

Figure 9. (a) Isolation, return loss, and insertion losses of the designed 4 × 4 Butler matrix obtained through 3D FEM simulations in ADS with Port 1 or Port 4 excited. (b) Isolation, return loss, and insertion losses of the designed 4 × 4 Butler matrix the obtained through 3D FEM simulations in ADS with Port 2 or Port 3 excited.

The insertion loss between port 1 or 4 and ports 5, 6, 7, and 8 are between –7.5 dB and –8.8 dB. The insertion loss between port 2 or 3 and ports 5, 6, 7, and 8 are between –7.4 dB and –10 dB. The return losses at respective ports are below –20 dB and isolation of adjacent input ports is below –20 dB.

E. 4 × 4 Butler Matrix Beampatterns

A microstrip antenna array is designed to validate the beamforming capability of the designed 4 × 4 Butler matrix. Figure 10 shows the 4 × 4 Butler matrix layout with inset-fed microstrip antenna array of four elements. The antenna design dimensions are provided in Table V. The dimensions of microstrip inset fed antenna are also found by repetitive iterations of parametric optimization in ADS.

TABLE V DIMENSIONS OF MICROSTRIP INSET FED ANTENNA

Parameter	d_{feed}	d	L_{feed}	L_a
Values(mm)	1.945	1.126	0.843	0.945

Parameter	S	W_a	W_f	W_{in}
Values(mm)	0.187	0.819	0.163	0.118

*All values are in mm.

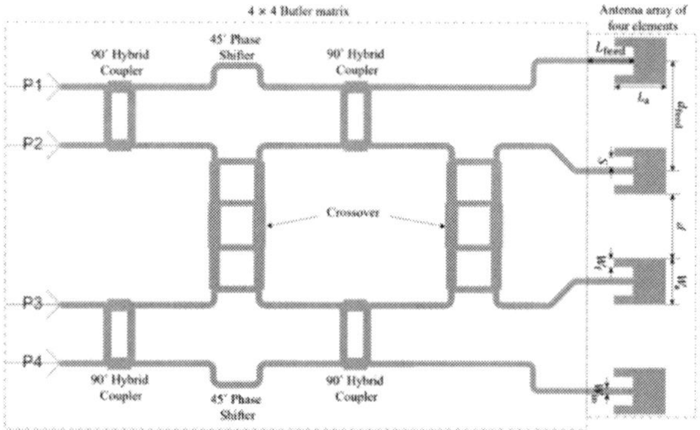

Figure 10. Layout of the complete 4 × 4 Butler matrix with antenna array

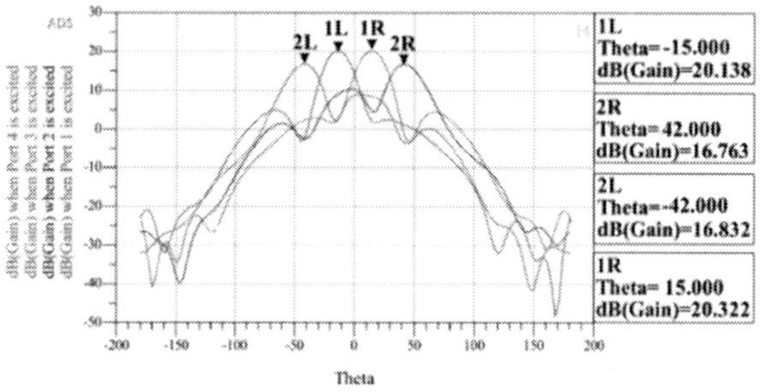

Figure 11. Rectangular plot of beamforming by the designed 4 × 4 Butler matrix.

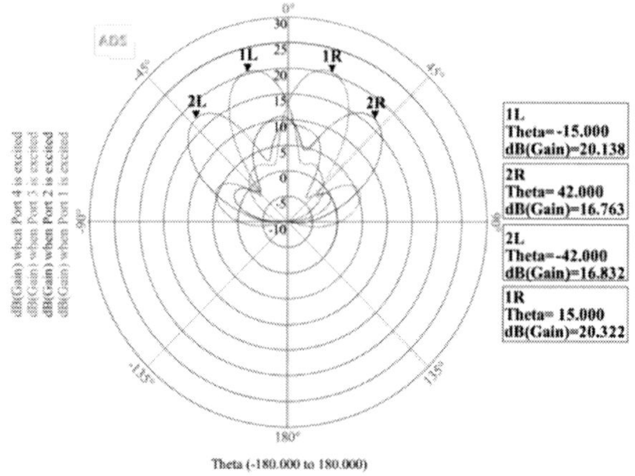

Figure 12. Polar plot of beamforming by the designed 4 × 4 Butler matrix.

When input ports 1, 2, 3 and 4 are excited individually, the beam patterns are observed at θ = –15°, 42°, –42° and

15°, respectively for azimuth angle (φ) = 90° as shown in Figure 11 and Figure 12. The beam angle phase error is ±7° from the expected beam angle phase given in Table 1. The maximum gain of 20.322 dB is observed on excitation of port 4. The minimum gain of 16.763 dB is observed on excitation of port 2. The difference between main lobe level and side lobe levels is higher than 14 dB when port 1 (or 1L) and port 4 (or 1R) is excited but lower than 10 dB when port 2 (or 2R) and port 3 (or 2L) are excited.

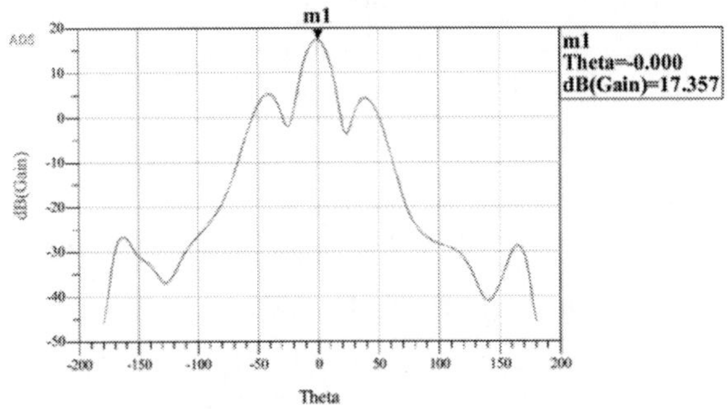

Figure 13. Rectangular plot of a beam pattern when all input ports of the designed 4 × 4 Butler matrix are excited.

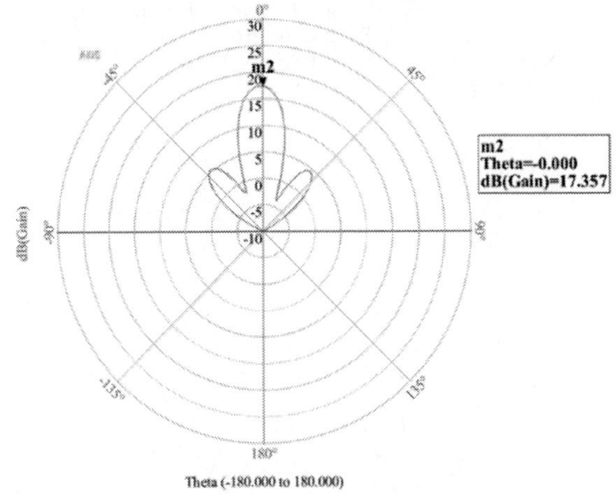

Figure 14. Polar plot of a beam pattern when all input ports of the designed 4 × 4 Butler matrix are excited.

When all the input ports are excited, the signal is received at output ports with $\Delta\phi = 0°$ and hence, the beam pattern is observed at $\theta = 0°$ as shown in Figure 13 and Figure 14. The respective gain of the main lobe is 17.357 dB. The difference between main lobe level and side lobe levels is significantly more than 11 dB.

III. CONCLUSION

The designed 77 GHz microstrip 4 × 4 Butler matrix on a 0.2 mm thick HPFS glass substrate has the potential to provide superior performance at a lower cost, smaller size, and thickness to realize compact radars to improve road safety and driving comfort for vehicles with advanced driver-assistance system (ADAS) and autonomous vehicles. It was observed that the glass substrate from Corning™ has superior loss characteristics to minimize insertion loss at high frequencies. However, optimization of the phase characteristics and insertion losses in a 3D FEM simulation environment requires more than 500 GB of memory. The time taken by ADS solvers to run one simulation is computationally extensive. Further optimization is necessary to improve the insertion loss and the phase error. Initial investigation shows that the device can be fabricated using a standard microfabrication technique, such as the lift-off process available in any standard microfabrication facility. The device will be fabricated and tested once the optimization process is completed.

ACKNOWLEDGEMENT

This research work was supported by the Natural Science and Engineering Research Council of Canada (NSERC)'s discovery grant number RGPIN 293218. The authors also acknowledge the collaborative research support provided by the IntelliSense Corporation, Lynnfield, MA, Angstrom Engineering, ON, and the CMC Microsystems, Canada.

REFERENCES

[1] J. Hasch, et al, "Millimeter-Wave Technology for Automotive Radar Sensors in the 77 GHz Frequency Band," in IEEE Trans. Microw. Theory and Techn., vol. 60, no. 3, pp. 845-860, March 2012, doi: 10.1109/TMTT.2011.2178427.

[2] S. Chatterjee, "A 77 GHz BCB Based High Performance Antenna Array for Autonomous Vehicle Radars," Electronic Theses and Dissertations. 7505, Dept. Elect. Comp. Eng., Univ. Windsor, Ontario, Canada.2018. [Online]. Available: https://scholar.uwindsor.ca/etd/7505. Retrieved: June, 2022.

[3] T. Wu, T. S. Rappaport, and C. M. Collins, "The human body and millimeter wave wireless communication systems: Interactions and implications," 2015 IEEE International Conference on Communications (ICC), London, UK, 2015, pp. 2423-2429, doi: 10.1109/ICC.2015.7248688.

[4] A. K. Vallappil, M. K. A. Rahim, B. A. Khawaja, N. A. Murad, and M. G. Mustapha, "Butler Matrix Based Beamforming Networks for Phased Array Antenna Systems: A Comprehensive Review and Future Directions for 5G Applications," in IEEE Access, vol. 9, pp. 3970-3987, 2021, doi: 10.1109/ACCESS.2020.3047696.

[5] J. Butler and R. Lowe. "Beam-forming matrix simplifies design of electronically scanned antennas." Electronic Design no.9, 1961, pp. 170-173.

[6] W. Rotman and R. Turner, "Wide-angle microwave lens for line source applications," in IEEE Trans. on Antennas and Propag., vol. 11, no. 6, pp. 623-632, November 1963, doi: 10.1109/TAP.1963.1138114.

[7] A. Attaran and S. Chowdhury, "Fabrication of a 77GHz Rotman Lens on a High Resistivity Silicon Wafer Using Lift-Off Process," in Int. J. Antennas and Propag., Vol 2014, Article ID 471935, pp. 1-9.

[8] J. Blass, "Multidirectional antenna - A new approach to stacked beams," in proc. of 1958 IRE Int. Conv. Rec., New York, NY, USA. 1960. pp. 48-50, doi: 10.1109/IRECON.1960.1150892.

[9] J. Nolen, "Synthesis of multiple beam networks for arbitrary illuminations," Ph.D. dissertation, Radio Division, Bendix Corp., Baltimore, MD, USA, Apr. 1965.

[10] H. Ren, H. Zhang, Y. Jin, Y. Gu, and B. Arigong, "A Novel 2-D 3×3 Nolen Matrix for 2-D Beamforming Applications," in IEEE Trans. on Microw. Theory and Techn., vol. 67, no. 11, pp. 4622-4631, Nov. 2019, doi: 10.1109/TMTT.2019.2917211.

[11] H. Nord, "Implementation of an 8x8-Butler Matrix in Microstrip", Diploma Thesis, Technische Universitat Wien, Vienna, Austria, 1998.

[12] R. D. Cerna and M. A. Yarlequé, "Design and implementation of a wideband 8x8 Butler Matrix for AWS and PCS 1900 MHz beamforming networks," in proc. of 2015 IEEE International Wireless Symposium (IWS 2015), Shenzhen, 2015, pp. 1-4, doi: 10.1109/IEEE-IWS.2015.7164630

[13] A. Shastrakar and U. Sutar, "Design and Simulation of Microstrip Butler Matrix Elements Operating at 2.4GHz for Wireless Applications", in Int. J. Scientific & Eng. Res., Volume 7, Issue 5, May-2016, pp. 1528-1531, ISSN 2229-5518.

[14] M. SalarRahimi and G. Vandenbosch, "Beam steerable subarray with small footprint for use as building block in wall-mounted indoor wireless infrastructure," IET Microw., Antennas & Propag., vol. 13, no. 4, pp. 526–531, Mar. 2019.

[15] T. Djerafi, N. Fonseca, and K. Wu, "Design and implementation of a planar 4x4 butler matrix in SIW technology for wideband applications," in proc. of The 40th European Microw. Conf., Paris, 2010, pp. 910-913, doi: 10.23919/EUMC.2010.5616642.

[16] H. Habibi, "Design of a 4x4 Butler Matrix for Vehicle Radar Beamforming Antenna systems at 24 GHz." Master's Thesis, Telecomunn. Eng. University of Gaza, Palestine, 2014.

[17] S. Orakwue, R. Ngah, T. Rahman, and H. Al-Khafaji, "A 4 × 4 Butler Matrix for 28 GHz Switched Multi-Beam Antenna," in Int. J. Eng. and Technol. (IJET), ISSN: 0975-4024, Vol 7 No 2, Apr-May 2015.

[18] I. Idrus, T. Latef, N. Aridas, and M. Talep, "Design and characterization of a compact single-layer multibeam array antenna using an 8x8 Butler matrix for 5G base station applications." in Turkish J. Electr. Eng. Comput. Sci. 28 (2020): pp. 1121-1134.2020.

[19] T. Djerafi and K. Wu, "A Low-Cost Wideband 77-GHz Planar Butler Matrix in SIW Technology," in IEEE Trans. on Antennas and Propag., vol. 60, no. 10, pp. 4949-4954, Oct. 2012, doi: 10.1109/TAP.2012.2207309.

[20] M. Rehman, S. Ravichandran, S. Erdogan, and M. Swaminathan, "W-band and D-band Transmission Lines on Glass Based Substrates for Sub-THz Modules," in proc. of 2020 IEEE 70th Electron. Compon. Techn. Conf. (ECTC), Orlando, FL, USA, 2020, pp. 660-665, doi: 10.1109/ECTC32862.2020.00109.

[21] Corning HPFS® Fused Silica. Datasheet, Corning Inc., May 2017. [Online] Available: https://www.corning.com/media/worldwide/csm/documents/CorningHPFSFusedSilicaWafer_PI.pdf. Retrieved: June, 2022

[22] Y. Uemichi, et al, "A ultra low-loss silica-based transformer between microstrip line and post-wall waveguide for millimeter-wave antenna-in-package applications," in proc. of 2014 IEEE MTT-S Int. Microw. Symp. (IMS2014), Tampa, FL, USA, 2014, pp. 1-3, doi: 10.1109/MWSYM.2014.6848279.

[23] Y. Uemichi, et al, "Characterization of 60-GHz silica-based post-wall waveguide and low-loss substrate dielectric," in proc. of 2016 Asia-Pacific Microw. Conf. (APMC), New Delhi, India, 2016, pp. 1-4, doi: 10.1109/APMC.2016.7931433.

Development of Sensor Devices for Structural Health Monitoring of Buildings and Civil Infrastructures

Narito Kurata
Faculty of Industrial Technology
Tsukuba University of Technology
Tsukuba City, Ibaraki, Japan
e-mail: kurata@home.email.ne.jp

***Abstract* - This paper reports the results of health monitoring of a building in Battleship Island and a structure of Angkor Wat, registered as World Heritage Sites. In addition, necessary functions for structural health monitoring of World Heritage are listed, and research on desirable sensor device is described. Specifically, the development of an autonomous time synchronization sensor equipped with a Chip Scale Atomic Clock (CSAC) that can hold accurate time information is reported.**

Keywords-Time Synchronization; Chip Scale Atomic Clock; Earthquake Observation; Structural Health Monitoring; Micro Electro Mechanical Systems; World Heritage

I. INTRODUCTION

Hashima Island in Nagasaki City in the south of Japan was registered as a World Cultural Heritage in 2015 [1]. The island was an offshore city that prospered as an undersea coal mine from the 1800s, and had a population density higher than that of Tokyo. The shape of the island resembles that of a battleship, so it is also referred to as "Battleship Island". Also, the World Heritage Site of Angkor Wat is part of the Angkor Ruins located in the northwestern part of Cambodia [2]. The structures registered as heritage sites are expected to be maintained and managed for centuries. However, heritage sites are subject to serious crises that damage these universal values, including armed conflict, natural disasters, large-scale construction, urban development, tourism development, and commercial poaching. To maintain and manage World Heritage Structures, an understanding of the condition should be obtained by monitoring heritage sites. Monitoring should be performed in accordance with the environmental needs and circumstances of each site.

In this paper, we develop an autonomous time-synchronization sensing system on which a Chip Scale Atomic Clock (CSAC) is mounted as an ideal sensing system to maintain high-precision absolute time information [3] [4]. Even if the CSAC-mounted sensor module/data logger is installed over a wide area and at high density, it is possible to acquire measurement data with time synchronization without relying on a network or a GPS signal. In this paper, examples of health monitoring at Battleship Island and Angkor Wat and the research and development of the CSAC-mounted sensor module are introduced.

Section II and Ⅲ show the results of structural health monitoring of a building in Battleship Island and a structure of Angkor Wat, respectively. Further, Section IV describes necessary functions for structural health monitoring of World Heritage are listed, and research and development of desirable sensor device is described.

II. MONITORING OF A BUILDING IN BATTLESHIP ISLAND

A. *No.3 Building of Battleship Island*

No. 3 Building on Battleship Island, shown in Figure 1, is a 4-story reinforced concrete housing complex constructed in 1959. It is located at the highest point on Battleship Island, and is a symbolic building that has a silhouette similar to that of a battleship. The building is relatively new on the island, with little sign of aging and damage. On the rooftop of No.3 Building, a wireless antenna for maritime radio communication with the Battleship Island Museum on the opposite shore, a solar panel, a storage battery, and cameras that capture images of the surrounding area, are installed. These serve as communication bases for the monitoring system.

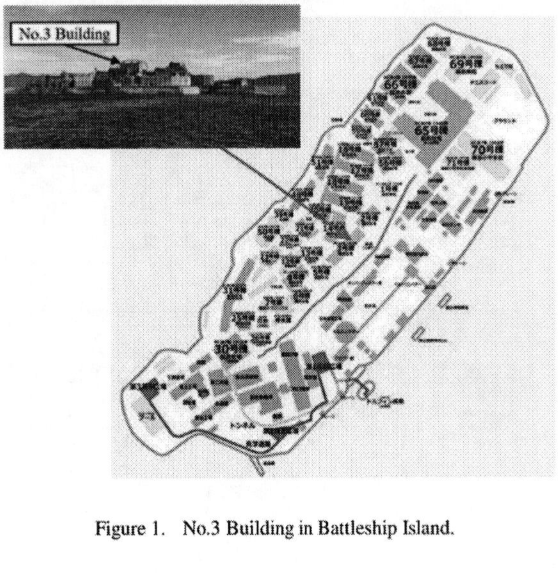

Figure 1. No.3 Building in Battleship Island.

B. Vibration Measurement System

Figure 2 shows the locations of the accelerometers in No. 3 Building. No. 3 Building has a flat, rectangular shape, with a total of 10 acceleration sensors installed on both sides of each floor. The accelerometers used are JA-70SA manufactured by Japan Aviation Electronics Industry. This accelerometer can measure a wide range of vibrations from microtremors, to strong vibrations during a typhoon or large earthquake. For vibration measurement, a data acquisition device (referred to as a DAQ) having a 16-channel A/D conversion module is used, and synchronization is performed to within 5 μsec by a multiplexer at the preceding stage. Time synchronization is performed by GPS, and the sampling frequency is set to 100Hz. A continuous measurement function that saves 10 minutes of measurement data every 2 hours and a trigger function that stores measurement data when more than a certain level of vibration occurs due to a typhoon or an earthquake are installed. The data stored in the data recorder is transmitted to a data server in the Battleship Island Museum on the opposite shore by a maritime radio communications antenna installed on the rooftop. This data server is accessible via the Internet. Solar panels and storage batteries are installed on the rooftop of the structure to serve as a power source for the vibration measurement system. PCs, the DAQ and accelerometers consume higher power, but they use system power efficiently to provide constant remote monitoring and continuous measurement.

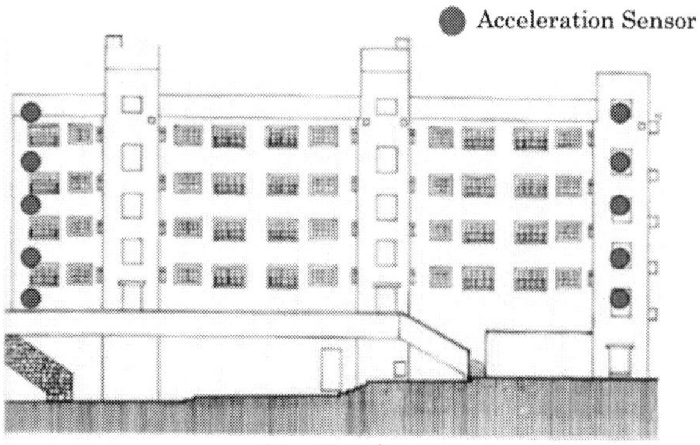

(a) Elevation

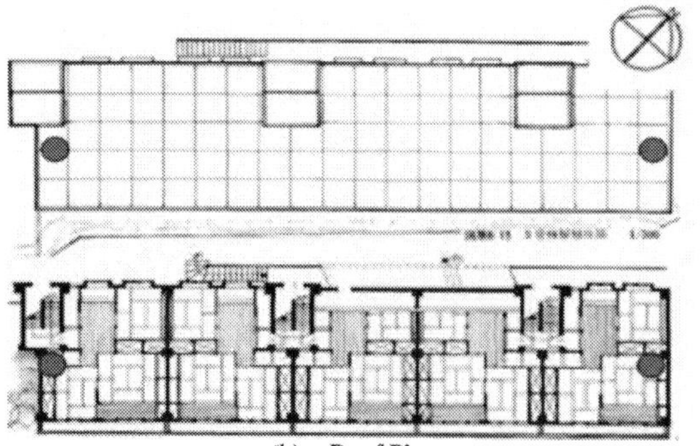

(b) Roof Plan

Figure 2. Sensor location.

C. Analytical Results of vibration

Figure 3 and 4 show amplitude ratios of Fourier acceleration spectra on the rooftop and the first floor calculated from acceleration data measured for 10 minutes from 12:00 every day, from June 1 to October 18, 2019. As can be seen from the figures, some parts of the data from August 12 to 19 and August 27 to 28 during the measurement period are missing. In each figure, the measurement dates, frequencies, and ratios of Fourier spectra are displayed in 3D and 2D. In addition, the dates of occurrence of three typhoons that caused strong vibrations in No. 3 Building during the measurement period are shown. Figure 3 shows the analysis results of the long-side components of the sensors installed on the south sides of No. 3 Building. From these figures, it can be seen that the first characteristic frequency clearly appears around 6 Hz during strong winds or a typhoon. In addition, characteristic frequencies of higher-order modes can be observed near 17 Hz. Further, if vibration of the building increases due to strong winds or a typhoon, vibration in the high frequency region of 10 Hz or more increases on the south side.

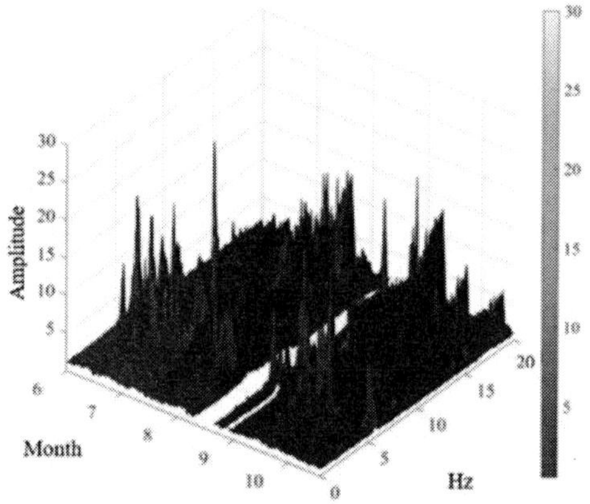

(a) South side (3D)

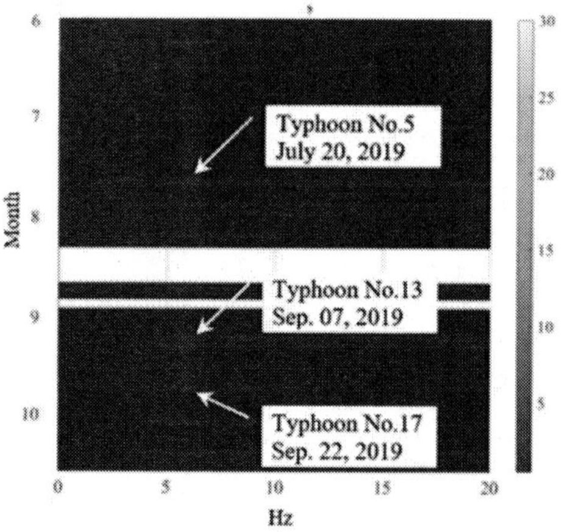

(b) South side (2D)

Figure 3. Fourier amplitude spectrum ratios of the acceleration data (Long-side component)

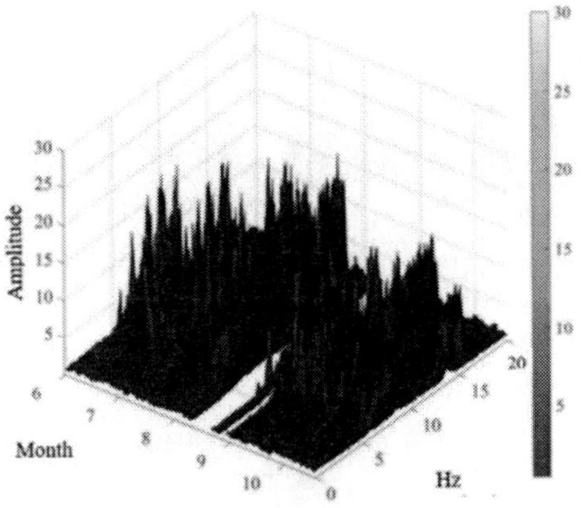

(a) South side (3D)

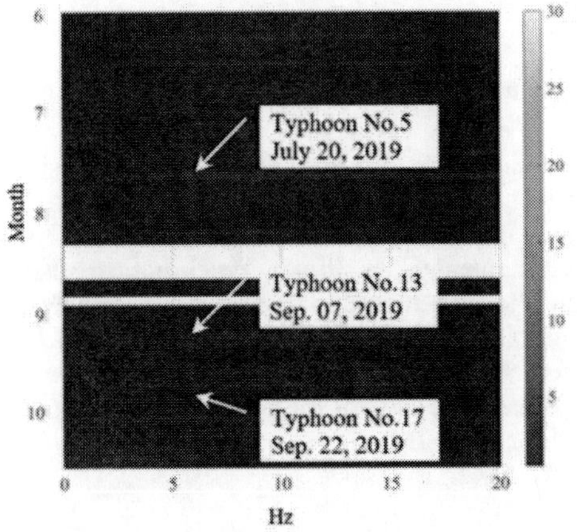

(b) South side (2D)

Figure 4. Fourier amplitude spectrum ratios of the acceleration data (Long-side component)

Figure 4 shows the analysis results of the short-side components of the sensors installed on the south sides of No. 3 Building. From these figures, it can be seen that characteristic frequencies appear at around 9 Hz and 14 Hz in addition to 6 Hz during strong winds or a typhoon. Further, when vibration of the building increases due to strong winds or a typhoon, the vibration on the south side is larger than that on the north side, and on the south side, vibration in the high frequency region of 10 Hz or more increases.

III. MONITORING OF A STRUCTURE OF ANGKOR WAT

A. *Angkor Wat*

The World Heritage Site of Angkor Wat (Figure 5) is part of the Angkor Ruins located in the northwestern part of Cambodia. The structure is a Hindu temple, and is regarded as a masterpiece of Khmer architecture. An image of the structure is displayed in the center of the Cambodian flag. The premises are surrounded by moats that are 1,500 meters in length from east to west, 1,300 meters in length from north to south, and 190 meters wide. The premises were mainly constructed from sandstone and laterite, and the temple was built by utilizing steelmaking technology in a nearby area. The structures are surrounded by a three-storied corridor. The first story corridor is 200 meters in length from east to west, and 180 meters in length from north to south. The second story corridor is 115 meters in length from east to west, and 100 meters in length from north to south. The third story corridor is 60 meters long on each side, and 13 meters higher than the second story corridor. To enter the third story corridor, it is necessary to climb a steep set on stone steps. In this corridor, five ancestral halls are located in each of the four corners and in the center; the central ancestral hall is 65 meters high.

Figure 5. Angkor Wat World Heritage Site.

B. *Measurement of Vibration*

As shown in Figure 6, a constant tremor was measured every 10 minutes at each location point (●) of the first, second, and third corridors of Angkor Wat. Measurements were taken with the single portable high-sensitivity acceleration sensor shown in Figure 7. The sampling frequency is 100 Hz. Measurements at the first and third story corridors are shown in Figure 8.

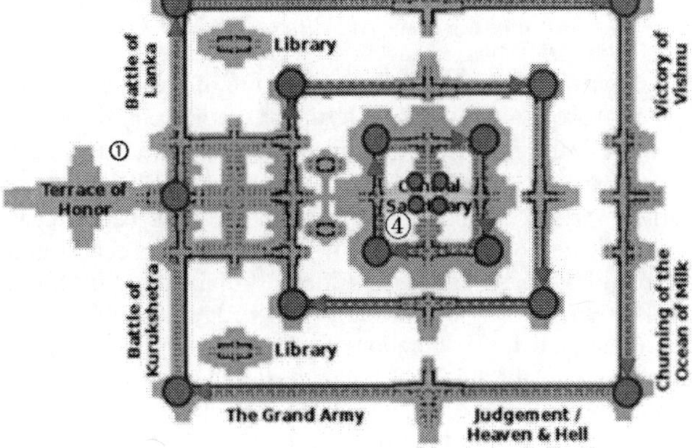

Figure 6. Floor plan and measurement points of Angkor Wat.

Figure 7. Portable acceleration sensor.

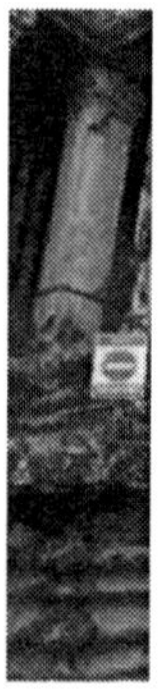

(a) The third corridor

(b) The first corridor

Figure 8. Measurement at the third and first corridor.

C. *Measurement at the Thrid Story Corridor*

Figure 9 shows the Fourier spectrum of the accelerogram as measured in the southwestern part of the central tower in the third story corridor (Figure 6, ④ part). Each figure is comprised of north-south (NS), east-west (EW), and up-down vertical direction(UD) components. Frequency peaks are indicated by blue and yellow arrow marks in each figure. Vibrations of 7-8 Hz are considered to be caused by tourist traffic on the stairs externally attached to the third story corridor, and local vibrations. It has been inferred that the structures in the third story corridor of Angkor Wat have a natural frequency of around 3 Hz. Structures resembling a rigid rocky mountain can be seen in the three-storied corridor.

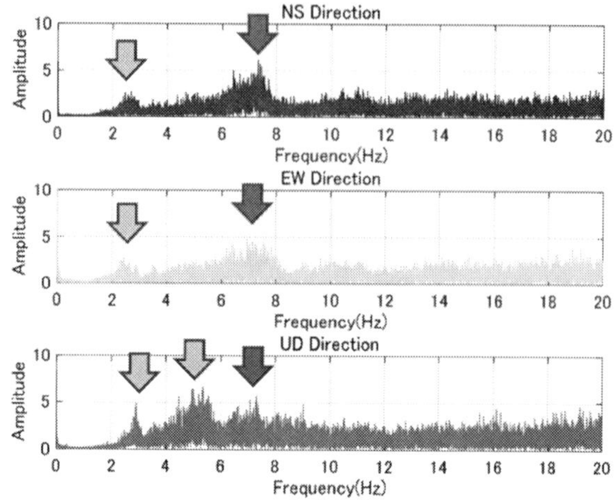

Figure 9. Fourier spectrum of the measured acceleration.

If the natural frequency moves to the lower side, rigidity will be lost, and structural deterioration and damage can be evaluated. In order to accurately evaluate this kind of natural frequency, a time synchronous measurement between the structure and the ground surface should be performed; a division of the frequency domain is required. Measurements should also be taken at the tops of the five ancestral halls (at each of the four corners and the center of the corridor).

IV. Future Direction on World Heritage Monitoring and the Need for Development of Senser Device

Battleship Island and Angkor Wat are typical sightseeing spots that bustles with tourists throughout the year. Therefore, there is heavy damage from tourist traffic in addition to age and deterioration. In order to evaluate the damage, data acquisition and accumulation by constant monitoring or periodic measurement is required. However, under the circumstances, it is not practical to bring in a large energy supply system or to wire the site for the purpose of taking measurements. Therefore, battery-driven sensor devices and data collection methods that are performed without wires are necessary. As well, Micro Electro Mechanical System (MEMS) based sensors that pursue low power consumption and involve high precision will be essential [5].

Furthermore, in order to carry out a highly accurate analysis, it is desirable to take multipoint measurements on the ground surface, at all three stories of the corridor, and on the ancestral halls for Angkor Wat. By simply installing sensors, it is possible to obtain autonomously accurate time information; the technology is expected to perform activities such as acquiring a data group that ensures time synchronization [3, 4]. These measures are also useful for monitoring the site for the management and maintenance of general building structures and social infrastructure. With the application of these methods to World Heritage monitoring in mind, research on the development of an autonomous time synchronization sensor module that holds highly accurate time information has been carried forward by using the CSAC. In order to acquire measurement data that secures time synchronization by installing the sensor devices in a wide area of high density, the sensor module itself should autonomously hold accurate time information without relying on a network or GPS signal. Therefore, a sensing module that autonomously holds accurate time information by mounting the CSAC has been developed (Figures 10 and 11).

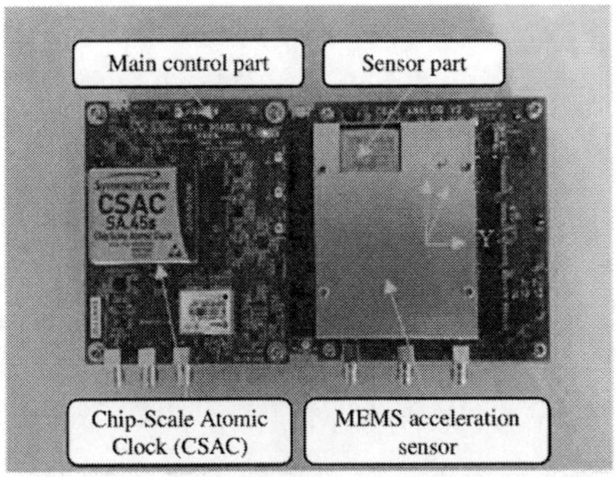

Figure 10. CSAC and sensor board.

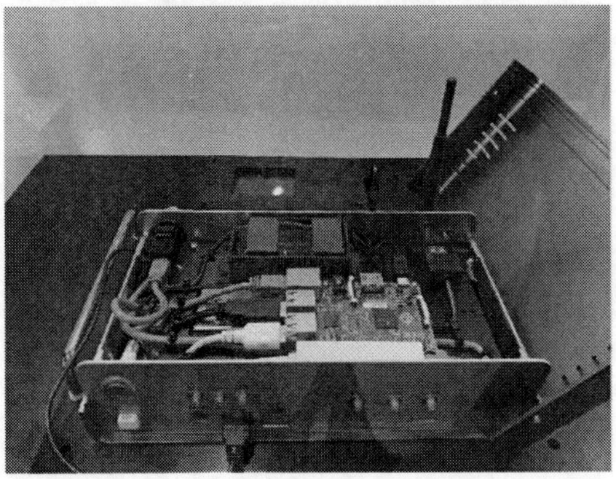

Figure 11. Sensor module.

The CSAC is an ultrahigh precision atomic clock that features ultra-low power consumption and ultra-small size, and can be mounted on-board. The module includes the CSAC in addition to the CPU, memory, storage, 3-axis MEMS acceleration sensor, external part analog sensor input interface, temperature sensor, anti-aliasing filter, and A/D converter. It is also equipped with a Field-Programmable Gate Array (FPGA), which is a dedicated integrated circuit that is used so time information from the CSAC can be directly sent to the sensor's measurement data. Although an Ethernet network interface has been provided for data communication, Wi-Fi and 3G/LTE communication functions have been separately added to improve the module's convenience as a sensor device. By developing this kind of autonomous time synchronization sensor module, a health monitoring application has been added to the structure. Furthermore, the developed sensor device was installed on actual buildings and bridges, and applied to seismic observation and evaluation of structural health.

Figure 12. Digital sensing platform.

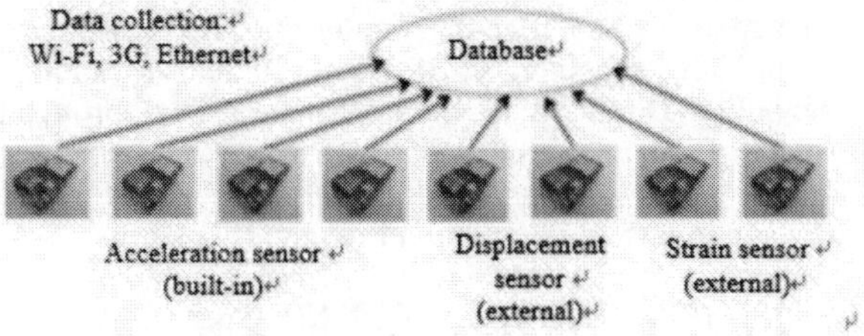

Figure 13. Autonomous time synchronization sensing system.

However, the MEMS acceleration sensor was mounted in the developed sensor device, so it was difficult to measure down to microtremors with high accuracy. The developed sensor device is equipped with an external analog input interface, through which any analog sensor can be connected. High-performance servo acceleration sensors can also be connected, but the risk of noise being mixed into the analog signal remains. Therefore, it was decided that a fully-fledged digital sensing platform (Figure 12) was developed. Specifically, a high-accuracy digital acceleration sensor was mounted in the sensor device to enable accurate acceleration measurements with no risk of noise being mixed in, and technology has been developed to add an accurate time stamp to the digital sensor output using CSACs.

In order to properly maintain and manage World Heritage for centuries by collecting, accumulating, and analyzing the measurement data, it is necessary to develop a sustainable database that copies the entire structure and ruins area from real space to cyberspace in addition to the development of a sensor and communications research

(Figure 13). Ultimately, it will be required to construct a Cyber-Physical Systems (CPS) of a World Heritage. The CPS of this sort can perform real-time sensing, event analysis, and prediction by big data assimilation, and can also control the real space of a site based on those results.

V. CONCLUSION

In this paper, the results of vibration measurement and data analysis of the structures at Battleship Island and Angkor Wat were reported. Structures registered as World Heritage Sites are expected to require maintenance and management for centuries. To maintain and manage a World Heritage structure, it is necessary to obtain knowledge of its status by suitably monitoring the environment in accordance with the structure's circumstances. Furthermore, the future direction on World Heritage monitoring and the need for the development of sensor device were discussed and research and development relating to a sensor device that autonomously retains highly accurate time information by applying a CSAC, was reported.

ACKNOWLEDGMENT

Nagasaki City cooperated with the installation and measurement on the Battleship Island. The photos were taken with the special permission of Nagasaki City. Measurements at Angkor Wat were supported by Mr. Mitsuo Ishizuka of the JASA/UNESCO project office. This research was partially supported by the New Energy and Industrial Technology Development Organization (NEDO) through the Project of Technology for Maintenance, Replacement and Management of Civil Infrastructure, Cross-ministerial Strategic Innovation Promotion Program (SIP). This research was also partially supported by JSPS KAKENHI Grant Number JP19K04963 and ROIS NII Open Collaborative Research 2022-22S0602.

REFERENCES

[1] World Heritage Committee, *Decisions adopted by the World Heritage Committee at its 39th session (Bonn, 2015).* [Online]. Available from: https://whc.unesco.org/document/139179 2015.11.19

[2] Charles River Editors, Angkor Wat: The History and Legacy of the World's Largest Hindu Temple, Createspace Independent Pub, 2017.

[3] N. Kurata, "An Autonomous Time Synchronization Sensor Device Using a Chip Scale Atomic Clock for Earthquake Observation and Structural Health Monitoring" The Eighth International Conference on Sensor Device Technologies and Applications (SENSORDEVICES 2017) IARIA, Sep. 2017, pp.31-36, ISSN: 2308-3514, ISBN: 978-1-61208-581-4

[4] N. Kurata, "High-precision Time Synchronization Digital Sensing Platform Enabling Connection of a Camera Sensor" The Twelfth International Conference on Sensor Device Technologies and Applications (SENSORDEVICES 2021) IARIA, Nov. 2021, pp. 98-104, ISSN: 2308-3514, ISBN: 978-1-61208-918-8

[5] N. Kurata, S. Saruwatari, and H. Morikawa, "Ubiquitous structural monitoring using wireless sensor networks" 2006 International Symposium on Intelligent Signal Processing and Communications (ISPACS 2006), Dec. 2006, pp. 99-102, ISBN: 0-7803-9733-9